Palestine's Horizon

Palestine's Horizon

Toward a Just Peace

Richard Falk

PlutoPress
www.plutobooks.com

First published 2017 by Pluto Press
345 Archway Road, London N6 5AA

www.plutobooks.com

Copyright © Richard Falk 2017

The right of Richard Falk to be identified as the author of this work has been
asserted by him in accordance with the Copyright, Designs and Patents Act 1988.

British Library Cataloguing in Publication Data
A catalogue record for this book is available from the British Library

ISBN   978 0 7453 9975 1   Hardback
ISBN   978 0 7453 9974 4   Paperback
ISBN   978 1 7868 0075 6   PDF eBook
ISBN   978 1 7868 0077 0   Kindle eBook
ISBN   978 1 7868 0076 3   EPUB eBook

This book is printed on paper suitable for recycling and made from fully managed
and sustained forest sources. Logging, pulping and manufacturing processes are
expected to conform to the environmental standards of the country of origin.

Typeset by Stanford DTP Services, Northampton, England

Simultaneously printed in the United Kingdom and United States of America

May Dawn Finally Arrive for the People of Palestine

Contents

Acknowledgements

No political issue during the last decade has been as preoccupying and discouraging for me as the failure to find a sustainable and just peace for the Palestinian people. This book attempts to depict recent phases of this Palestinian struggle and its aspirations. It is also animated by the belief that history cannot be undone, and that a decent future depends on Palestinians and Israelis finding creative ways to live together that are beneficial for both peoples.

In preparing this book, I was greatly influenced by my six years (2008–2014) serving as the UN Special Rapporteur for the Palestinian Territories Occupied since 1967 under the auspices of the Human Rights Council. In that role, I was greatly assisted by several talented and energetic members of the staff of the Office of the High Commissioner for Human Rights in Geneva: Linnea Arvidsson, Kiyohiko Hasegawa, and Kevin Turner were particularly helpful in countless ways, including substantively.

Among Palestinians, I have benefited always from the insight, experience, and friendship of Raji Sourani and Mohammed Omer, who are brave and doing invaluable work under the most difficult of conditions. In the United States, I would mention Ali Abunimah, who has long contributed humane and engaged commentary on the Palestinian struggle, as well as being the founder and main coordinator of the online *Electronic Intifada* that offers one of the best sources of information about the ongoing developments arising from the daily friction of Israel/Palestine interaction.

There are many others who deserve mention, but to avoid a long list, I will mention only Jeff Halper and Phyllis Bennis, who are both dedicated to a just outcome of the long conflict that is responsive to Palestinian grievances and rights, while being mindful of Israel's security and survival.

Vicky Mason agreed to allow the inclusion here of our collaborative article on Palestinian nonviolence, and deserves the lion's share of the credit for the shaping and presentation of this generally overlooked dimension of Palestinian resistance. I also want to thank Norma Hashim for involving me in her important efforts to make available to the world the voices of Palestinian prisoners, including children, which are not only moving but also confirm impressions of the cruelty of Israel practices associated with its occupation regime.

It was my pleasure to work with Pluto Press from start to finish on this book. David Shulman was not only encouraging all along, but also made detailed and fundamental suggestions that led me to do considerable additional work on the manuscript for which I am deeply grateful. I would also like to thank Thérèse Wassily Saba for her incredibly careful copy-editing, which saved me from a series of awkward oversights and mistakes. I would thank also Auriol Griffith-Jones for her expert preparation of the index and Dave Stanford for so diligently overseeing the final stages of preparation.

As with all of my work and overall life experience, Hilal Elver has acted as my devoted and loving partner, while also managing to be my fiercest critic.

Richard Falk
Santa Barbara, California
December 16, 2016

Preface

As of the end of 2016, the future of the Israel–Palestine conflict seems poised to enter a new phase. On the one side, with impressive unanimity, the UN Security Council condemned Israeli settlement expansion in Resolution 2334 by a vote of 14:0, with the United States abstaining. This symbolic act confirmed that the major countries of the world remain committed to a fair outcome of the conflict, respectful of Palestinian rights under international law, and that the UN would continue to have a vital role to play in this process.

At the same time, the idea of achieving a sustainable peace in the form of the two-state solution, while remaining the official position at the UN and in diplomatic circles, seems as remote as ever from being realized. The current Israeli government seems uninterested in a negotiated compromise with representatives of the Palestinian people. Furthermore, the Palestinians lack unified leadership and do not presently possess entirely legitimate representation. Additionally, developments on the ground suggest an Israeli push to retain control of all of Jerusalem and most of the West Bank, making unrealistic the establishment of a viable and sovereign Palestinian state upon which the two-state approach rests.

In effect, although the Palestinian struggle on the international level, especially at the UN, continues, there is an almost total disbelief in either the proposed two-state solution or in the capacity of traditional diplomacy to create agreement between Israel and Palestine. Instead, what hope exists depends on shifting the current balance of forces so that the Israeli government is led to recalculate its interests in ways that make it possible to envision a fair and sustainable political accommodation with the Palestinian national movement. Such a shift, if it is to occur, will be a result of a reinvigorated Palestinian resistance to the Israeli occupation that is entering its 50th year and a growing global solidarity movement featuring the BDS (Boycott, Divestment, and Sanctions) Campaign designed to challenge Israeli policies and practices that violate international law. As this book argues, Palestinian prospects presently seems to rest on the activism of people rather than the diplomacy of governments and the United Nations. If the relation of forces changes to create more balance, a revived diplomacy based on a genuine peace process might contribute in the future to a solution.

These perspectives are explored in a series of thoroughly revised essays that have been written with this interpretation in mind. It begins with a cluster of chapters that sets forth the Palestinian imaginary, its agenda, and altered tactics in view of an overall political context in which the diplomatic framework that was established quite long ago to bring peace to Israel and Palestine has been deeply discredited after decades of frustration. In response to earlier failures of armed struggle and more recent frustrations of diplomacy, increasing attention is being given to civil society activism, both as Palestinian resistance to occupation and as global solidarity with the Palestinian struggle for self-determination and rights under international law.

The second section contains chapters highlighting this Palestinian strategic and tactical shift in emphasis that increasingly relies on a variety of nonviolent initiatives, internally and internationally, designed to expose, discredit, and challenge Israel's unlawful and immoral policies and practices. Whether such tactics can sufficiently alter the relation of forces that has been weighted so heavily in Israel's favor is the overriding question that will not be quickly resolved, and will in turn be influenced by how regional tensions in the Middle East are handled and by whether there will be any changes in approach to the conflict by either the United States or Europe.

The third section is devoted to Israel's vigorous response against these more recent Palestinian tactics by adopting a series of tactics of its own, including aggressive campaigns to smear BDS and other pro-Palestinian activists as "anti-Semites." This Israeli pushback avoids addressing the substantive challenges to its policies and practices, and concentrates its efforts on discrediting critics and activists, attacking the United Nations as biased, and relying on various forms of intimidation at home and internationally.

The fourth and final section is devoted to depicting different facets of Edward Said's vibrant, enduring legacy as the most influential and humane voice of the Palestinian people as an abidingly valuable source of humane reflection and guidance. It is notable that toward the end of his life Said placed his hopes on a one-state solution in which Palestinians and Israelis would live together in a single secular state that underpinned the equality of the two peoples by a strong commitment to uphold the human rights of all who lived within its borders. In important respects, the chapters contained in this volume can be read as an extended endorsement of and commentary upon the views so eloquently set forth by Edward Said.

PART I

PALESTINE'S EMERGENT IMAGINARY

I

Parameters of Struggle

Writing from the standpoint of 2017, it seems worth noting that in this year a converging series of anniversaries are calling renewed attention to some long past milestones in the Israel–Palestine conflict. These remembrances cast an explanatory light on the historical narrative that continues to unfold, and helps to avoid overlooking the relevance of past occurrences. Of these, the Balfour Declaration of 1917 underlines the long Zionist quest for a Jewish Homeland in Palestine, and it also calls our attention to the fact that this initial encouragement of the World Zionist Movement arose from a willingness of the British Foreign Secretary, Lord Alfred Balfour, to express an official show of support on behalf of his government. The Balfour Declaration was without doubt a colonial initiative that collided with competing nationalist ideas associated with every people's right of self-determination to be exercised in their place of geographic habitat. In this regard, and arguably ever since, the West has given support to the Zionist project without ever either taking into account these colonialist origins or making any effort to assess the preferences and views of the indigenous population as it existed in 1917. True, the Balfour Declaration contained language that reassured the non-Jewish inhabitants of Palestine that their rights should not be jeopardized as a result of the pro-Zionist pledge, although the clause received almost no subsequent notice. It should also be noted that the Balfour Declaration looked toward the establishment of a Jewish "homeland" in Palestine, making no reference one way or the other to the establishment of a state, let alone a Jewish state. In this regard, the establishment of the state of Israel in 1948 went beyond the explicit endorsement of Zionist goals in the Balfour Declaration, disclosing an expansionist pattern that persists up to the present. In other words, the Zionist project is dynamic, expanding its goals to take advantage of increased capabilities and opportunities.

A second anniversary is associated with the backing of the United Nations in 1947 for a partition of Palestine into two political communities, one for Jews and the other for Arabs. This UN initiative, taking the form of General Assembly Resolution 181, took place 60 years ago, abandoning the idea of a unified country of the sort administered by the United Kingdom in the mandates system after the collapse of the Ottoman Empire in the aftermath of World War I. The partition approach was adopted after Britain voluntarily terminated its governing role in Palestine due to the growing unmanageability of the situation, dramatized by violent and escalating efforts of Zionist militias to make the British presence untenable. This idea of partition became the internationally agreed basis for a solution to the conflict ever since 1947, giving rise in recent decades to the two-state consensus that was at the core of the failed effort of Oslo diplomacy to end the conflict. As of 2017, questions arise as to whether Israel continues to endorse partition if it means the emergence of an independent Palestinian state. Regardless of Israel's outlook, the two-state approach no longer seems a practical possibility in view of the scale and geographic breadth of the settler movement that continues to expand within the confines of Occupied Palestine. Among Palestinians there persists uncertainty, with the formal international representation of the Palestinian people by way of the Palestinian Authority and the Palestinian Liberation Organization (PLO), adhering to its central demands to end the occupation by withdrawing its forces, and allowing the present "ghost state" of Palestine to assume real governing authority. Palestinian civil society voices are more agnostic about their hopes and demands, often opting for the restoration of a unified secular Palestine with equality for all ethnicities and religions as the preferred solution.

A third milestone is associated with the 50th anniversary of the 1967 War, that converted a situation of de facto partition into one of Israel's control over the whole of Palestine, due to its belligerent occupation and effective control over the West Bank, East Jerusalem, and Gaza. The international community insisted in 1967 that these new circumstances arising from the war should be temporary. Israel was expected to withdraw as a matter of obligation under international law, although the process was to be facilitated by way of minor adjustments in the pre-1967 borders. These expectations were embedded in UN Security Resolution 242, unanimously adopted, and the beginning of the view that peace depended on restoring prospects for a legally agreed upon partition in a manner that would give Palestine an independent sovereign state. As the years have passed, it has become less and less likely that the path to peace foreshadowed by Resolution 242 will ever be taken. Israel has demonstrated the will and capabilities to retain control over the whole of Palestine, a position made tenable by the unconditional geopolitical backing that Israel has received from the United States.

One major result of the 1967 War, which has never changed during the ensuing decades, was to shift Israel from its earlier status as a strategic burden of the United States into its new role as valued strategic partner. This shift, reinforced by the 9/11 attacks on the United States, undoubtedly strengthened the special relationship between Israel and the United States with the effect of rendering Washington too partisan to serve as a diplomatic intermediary credible to the Palestinian side. Israel's influence and the USA's global leadership were translated into an unbalanced negotiating framework. All subsequent diplomatic initiatives gave the United States, despite its partisan connection with Israel, this important third-party role as a supposed honest broker. Palestinian frustrations with such a diplomatic process were to be expected, as progress toward a peaceful solution seemed permanently stalled while Israel continued full speed ahead in pursuit of its territorial ambitions in Occupied Palestine. The discussion of the diplomacy that was generated by the outcome of the 1967 War gave the false impression that the conflict could be reduced to a territorial dispute, overlooking the plight of Palestinian refugees seeking an end to their ordeal consistent with international law.

Interpreting these anniversaries provides a helpful perspective on the present, and on how it has come to pass in response to a series of developments over the course of an entire century. Additionally, there is something new and unpredictable upon the political horizon in 2017—the advent of the presidency of Donald J. Trump. During the presidential campaign, Trump spoke in generalities about his unbounded enthusiasm for Israel, and by his silence, indicated a lack of empathy for Palestinian rights and aspirations. In a typically contra-dictory spirit, Trump also suggested that his prowess as a deal-maker could be brought into play through a renewed attempt to find a solution acceptable to both Israelis and Palestinians. The most likely possibility is that the opportunistic side of Trump's political profile will incline him toward an acceptance of Israel's unilateral approach, which seeks to exert unified control over most of the West Bank, if not its totality, as well as to maintain governing authority over the entire city of Jerusalem, and a willingness to let go of Gaza, preferably to be governed in the future by Egypt or possibly Jordan. Trump seemed inclined toward satisfying Israeli political ambitions when he indicated that he favored moving the American Embassy from Tel Aviv to Jerusalem, which would be a major political gift to Israel, a strong irritant to Palestine, and indeed, the entire Muslim world, and an act done in defiance of world public opinion. What seems likely is that the Trump impact will shake the settled pattern of relations between Israelis and Palestinians, as well as impacting upon the various centers of regional turmoil throughout the Middle East. Trump's unpredictability makes it premature to anticipate the effects of his presidency beyond these generalities.

Against this background, there are four features of the Palestinian struggle that are currently salient: (1) the breakdown of any credible effort to reach a diplomatic outcome by negotiations between Israel and the Palestinian Authority, and hence widespread disillusionment about the prospects of making progress toward realizing the still internationally endorsed "two-state solution"; (2) the persisting dual reality of Palestinian suffering extending into the future without any discernible endpoint and continuing Israeli encroachment on Palestinian rights, including the progressive incorporation of land on territories occupied since the end of the 1967 War; (3) the growing global solidarity movement centered upon the BDS Campaign coupled with Israeli pushback by way of conflating mounting pressures on Israel with anti-Semitism; and (4) a regional political setting that has temporarily marginalized the Palestinian struggle due to a preoccupation with the ongoing carnage in Syria and Yemen, as well as the resultant refugee crisis and the rise of ISIS.

The wider context of Palestine–Israel relations reinforces these dominant features. The intensifying turmoil in the Middle East seems to strengthen Israel's evident satisfaction with a status quo that does not impede its expansionist policies and practices. As suggested, this shift of regional and world attention to the challenges posed by the rise and spread of ISIS, the continuing strife in Syria as abetted by outside interventions by Russia, Iran, the United States, and others, the Saudi intervention in Yemen, as well as chaos in Iraq and Libya, the various Kurdish involvements, all of this further complicated by the sectarian encounter between Saudi Arabia and Iran in several national and regional theaters of conflict. These developments have shifted priorities for all political actors in the region in such a way as to weaken significantly concern and identification with the Palestinian struggle. In the case of Saudi Arabia, this shift has been so drastic as to create a tacit alliance with Israel, or at minimum a convergence of interests, as was evident during the 2014 Israeli attack on Gaza during which Saudi Arabia gave at least support through its diplomatic silence.

Israel has also been a beneficiary of several other developments leaving them a free hand to deal with Palestine and Palestinians without any need to exhibit accountability to international law or respect for the authority of the United Nations. Egypt's resurgent authoritarianism since the military coup of 2013 has restored a collaborative relationship with Israel that is even stronger than what existed during the period of Mubarak rule. Beyond this, Turkey's preoccupations with renewed armed confrontations with its large Kurdish minority, as well as the various spillovers from the Syrian civil war has given Ankara's leaders more than they can handle, which explains the weakening of their support for the Palestinian struggle as well as a willingness to normalize relations with Israel. And even Iran, while not abandoning its rhetorical hostility to Israel, has made it evident that its present priority is to improve relations with the West, ending its isolation, and gaining relief from international sanctions that have had such a crippling effect on the Iranian economy and caused the Iranian people many hardships.

Despite the personality and policy clashes between Netanyahu and Obama, the "special relationship" between Israel and the United States has held firm. In effect, this posture of unconditional support gives Israel the political space to pursue its ambitions to colonize what is left of historic Palestine. The harshest words that Washington utters in response to continuing Israeli settlement expansion is to call such blatantly unlawful behavior "unhelpful," which in diplomatic parlance amounts to nothing more than "a slap on the wrist." Looking to the future, there is no daylight whatsoever separating the presidential candidates when it comes to future relations with Israel, which promise to be at best, more of the same, and likely will try to restore harmony at the leadership levels regardless of who is the president after Obama, although the primary campaign of Bernie Sanders to become the candidate of the Democratic Party disclosed a split among Jews, and briefly suggested a potential future repositioning of the American relationship with Israel on the basis of "tough love." To be realistic, this kind of desirable future in American relations with Israel will not occur without a minor political miracle, which seems even more improbable given the early signs of what a Trump presidency is likely to do.

This top down view of the Palestinian situation is far from the whole story. Despite the persistence of an oppressive occupation Palestinian resistance continues, adopting a variety of forms that deprive Israel of living in "a comfort zone." The recent flurry of stabbings, hyperbolically described in some circles as "the Third Intifada," can be interpreted from different angles. It seems best explained as pathological and spontaneous expressions of existential despair among ordinary Palestinians, paralleled by an upsurge of suicides in Gaza that also are interpreted as representing a loss of hope among Palestinians. This unorganized renewal of Palestinian violent resistance can also be understood as a warning that a full-fledged resumption of armed struggle could occur if the Palestinian prospects for peace and self-determination do not markedly improve in the months and years ahead, which will take some doing considering the collapse of the Oslo diplomacy as aggravated by accelerated Israeli expansionism and the disinclination of Israel to lend any further credence to the two-state solution.

Longer term trends in the region are highly unpredictable, and with support for the Palestinians still intense among the Arab masses, the political mood of Arab leaders could quickly reverse course, confronting Israel with renewed military threats in an environment in which several governments now have the weapons and delivery systems capable of causing serious damage in Israel, although not without exposing themselves to annihilating retaliation.

Perhaps, more telling in the near future than the maneuvers of governments, is the steady growth of the global Palestinian solidarity movement, as stimulated by Palestinian civil society initiatives and led by diaspora Palestinians, and mobilizing increasing support throughout the world, especially in Europe and North America. In this respect, there is a growing recognition that the Boycott, Divestment, and Sanctions (BDS) Campaign is gaining momentum, and may have reached a tipping point in imposing tangible costs on the Israeli economy. Israeli think-tanks and leaders have voiced their concern about what has been described as "the delegitimation project," which has come to be regarded as a greater security threat to Israel than Palestinian armed resistance.

What is notable about this latest phase of the Palestinian struggle is its focus on gaining the high ground with respect to law and morality, and thereby prevailing in the "Legitimacy War" being waged on a variety of symbolic battlefields, including within various UN venues. Such a strategic orientation places great emphasis on international law, on UN assessments of rights and grievances, on world public opinion, on activism by prominent cultural and moral authority figures, on boycott initiatives of academic institutions and professional associations, and on disengagement in various ways by governments, corporate actors, and private and international financial institutions.

A stunning aspect of these various symbolic struggles is the realization that the political fate of national movements of self-determination has been overwhelming controlled by the winners of legitimacy wars ever since the end of World War II (although not before), rather than by the side that possesses military superiority.

If we look ahead in an effort to situate the Palestinian struggle, I believe we are now experiencing both a post-diplomatic mood of frustration and an emerging pre-diplomatic mood of expectation, although the latter seems conditional on a change of approach by both the United States/Europe and Israel, that is, on repositioning moves that would amount to a political miracle. This change would involve establishing a more balanced and neutral diplomatic framework than the decades of pro-Israeli one-sidedness that doomed the "Oslo peace process" to failure. It would also depend on a firm agreement among the main Palestinian political forces (PLO, Hamas, and possibly Islamic Jihad) on unified representation including participation by refugee communities, and likely the release of most Palestinian political prisoners being detained without charges and likely of Marwan Barghouti, a high-profile political leader long imprisoned, who alone among Palestinian leaders enjoys respect across factional lines.

2

Oslo Diplomacy:
A Legal Historical Perspective

Points of Departure

When the Oslo Accords were signed on September 13, 1993 and confirmed for the world with the famous handshake on the White House lawn between Yasir Arafat and Yitzhak Rabin with a smiling Bill Clinton looking on, many thought that finally the Israel–Palestine conflict was winding down, or at worst, entering its final phase. It seemed like there was a shared commitment between the parties, with strong backing by the United States, to strike a compromise more or less along the borders established by the 1948 armistice agreement that enlarged the Israeli territory from the 57 percent of the British mandate allocated for a Jewish homeland by the UN in General Assembly Resolution 181 to the 78 percent of Palestine held by Israel at the start of the 1967 War. The other issues in dispute, although deferred until the so-called final status negotiations including the arrangements governing Jerusalem, Palestinian refugees, Israeli settlements, permanent borders, water rights, and security guarantees were all widely assumed at the time to be capable of compromise and mutual acceptance. The Accords proposed resolution of these issues within five years, which then seemed reasonable, as was the commitment to begin final status negotiations no later than 1996.

From the perspective of the present, the prospect of peaceful resolution seems more elusive than ever, and indeed conditions have so adversely altered as to make any assertion of an attainable and sustainable peace seem to be at best an exercise in wishful thinking, and at worst, an expression of bad faith. How can we explain, then, the Oslo Accords, widely celebrated in 1993 as an historic breakthrough, now appearing to have been a roadblock that insidiously diverted the

Palestinian struggle for self-determination while granting time to Israel to expand its territorial claims and virtually extinguish any realistic prospect of realizing Palestinian rights in the near future. What can we learn from this experience? Were the Palestinians blind sided, or did the Palestinians themselves contribute to this overall weakening of their position by engaging in violent forms of resistance that gave Israel time, space, and world sympathies enabling the pursuit of expansionist ambitions? Or were the Palestinians insufficiently united behind the Oslo Accords to provide the needed political support for the necessary compromise implicit in the idea of legitimating Israel as a Jewish state?

And there were other issues that seem appropriate to raise after the passage of time. Did Israel overreach in such a way as to undermine their long-term security due to regional power shifts that make their situation more precarious than ever? It is important to appreciate that the technological progress in weaponry and doctrinal shifts in tactics makes all political actors, including those with apparent military dominance, vulnerable to devastating attacks. This is part of the lesson of the 9/11 attacks carried out with minimal capabilities and almost no material resources. What Israel has done is to create a seemingly irreversible situation in the occupied territories of the West Bank and East Jerusalem that has the collateral effect of depriving Tel Aviv of a peace option. The PLO in 1988, five years before Oslo, committed the Palestinians to such an option by accepting the existence of Israel within the 1948 armistice borders with the territorial remnant providing the basis for a Palestinian state that was significantly smaller than what the UN proposed in its partition plan, a plan had been disastrously rejected by Palestinians when put forward because it then seemed grossly unfair to the majority Arab Palestinian resident population. In a sense, the overarching question at present, after the collapse of Oslo diplomacy, is to assess whether this dismal conclusion that the peace option is now foreclosed for both sides is persuasive or not. And if so, what now?

Recovering the 1993 Outlook

It seemed to many of us that the secret discussions in Oslo that had produced this agreed framework for negotiations would steer the parties in the direction of a sustainable peace, but even at the outset there were skeptics and many good reasons for skepticism existed. To begin with, there was no reference made in the framework to Palestinian sovereign statehood as a stipulated goal of the process, and there was not even a reference to the Palestinian right of self-determination.

An even more serious omen of trouble ahead was the absence of a clear-cut political consensus on either side in support of the approach and assumptions embodied in the Oslo Accords. In retrospect, the Oslo Accords were more pleasing to Washington than to either of the parties as it seemed to dispose of the conflict in a manner that allowed the United States to realize its Grand Strategy of oil energy geopolitics in the region. In the Israeli Knesset, despite the Labor Government being in power, the vote on the Oslo Accords was too close for comfort, with 61 in favor, 50 opposed, and nine abstentions. The depth of Israeli opposition was disclosed by the assassination of Yitzhak Rabin in 1995 by Yigal Amir, a religious Jew associated with hard-core settler outlooks emboldened by biblical claims, thereby eliminating the most respected Israeli leader identified with the Oslo approach to Israel's future well-being. It is significant that Benjamin Netanyahu and his Likud Party were openly opposed to the Oslo Accords from the outset, and its implications of withdrawal and the ensuing establishment of a Palestinian state. Before Rabin's death, Netanyahu had attacked Rabin for his accommodationist views, accusing him of "being removed from Jewish traditions ... and Jewish values" at anti-Oslo rallies.[1] Such attitudes exhibited so provocatively within Israel were not expressed internationally as the pretense was maintained that all political tendencies in Israel were seeking a negotiated peace.

In addition, the Israeli electorate was drifting in a rightwards direction, which signaled political trouble ahead for the Oslo timetable and the overall negotiating process, and a reluctance to travel very far down the Oslo road. The Israeli ambivalence toward the Oslo Accords reflected the tension between those who sought a peace based on a two-state consensus and those who believed that Israel's destiny and security depended on the prevention of Palestinian statehood, and coupled this with the belief that all of Jerusalem and as much as possible of the West Bank should be incorporated into an expanded Israel that was biblically ordained. Netanyahu became prime minister of Israel between 1996 and 2002, followed by Ariel Sharon who lasted until his stroke in 2006, with Netanyahu's second period as Israel's leader commencing in 2009.[2]

On the Palestinian side there was also strong opposition to the partition implications of the Oslo process. It seemed to accept the two-state approach to achieving a peaceful solution of the conflict, which meant both legitimizing Israel and splitting Palestine in two. It also appeared to look toward a state based on the 1967 borders, as adjusted, rather than the partition proposed in General Assembly Resolution 181 that was significantly more generous to the Palestinians with respect to the division of the territory administered by the United Kingdom during their mandatory role in Palestine. Further, the dominant PLO position since 1988 seemed to over-territorialize the dispute, expressed by the formula "land for peace," thereby diluting the claims of those several million Palestinians living in refugee camps or being part of an involuntary diaspora.

The more militant Palestinian factions refused to endorse such a prospect, including Hamas, Islamic Jihad, and the Popular Front for the Liberation of Palestine. Many prominent Palestinian intellectuals, including Edward Said, felt that the partition approach based on ethnic states was doomed to failure from the perspective of a just peace, and that in any event an acceptance of the ethos of modernity required that all sovereign states be secular rather than politically enshrining an ethnic or religious identity.[3]

The argument against partition was that it would produce unequal polities given the power and diplomatic disparities between the parties, that it would subject the large Palestinian minority in Israel to permanent second-class citizenship, and that it would never produce a sustainable peace because it was totally unacceptable to those Palestinians who had fled or been forced from their homes and villages in the course of 1947–1948 war.

Arafat was clearly the most dominant leader among the Palestinians yet even he lacked the full support of the Palestinian people with respect to a peacemaking approach that was premised on the creation of two ethnic states. At best, Arafat's embrace of the Oslo Accords enjoyed fragile political support as many on the Palestinian side worried that refugee rights would be sacrificed given the eagerness of Arafat to achieve statehood or that the Israelis would not in the end agree to a reasonable compromise on the final status issues, taking account of their refusal to abate the settlement process, and their formal moves to annex and enlarge Jerusalem in defiance of the UN and the international consensus. These worries were reinforced by the power imbalance embedded in the diplomatic process to be followed: Israel was much stronger in negotiating capabilities and circumstances than the Palestinians and this disparity was greatly reinforced by the United States playing the mediating third-party role despite being the undisguised and unconditional ally of Israel. Indeed, it was an unmistakable sign of Palestinian weakness to have accepted this kind of framework, and not to have insisted at least on neutral auspices for further negotiations. Could one even imagine Israel accepting the auspices of the Arab League as the supposed honest broker in the negotiations? Actually, the American relationship was far closer than this reversal of third-party identity as the United States was a major donor and supplier of weaponry to Israel, as well as its strategic partner in the region, especially since the Israeli victory in the 1967 War.[4]

The historical timing of Oslo also seemed to maximize Israeli bargaining power as the Palestinian Liberation Organization (and Arafat) had badly miscalculated, backing Saddam Hussein's Iraq in the just concluded Gulf War, and thereby losing major diplomatic and financial support among Gulf countries. Once again the Palestinians found themselves backed against the wall. It seemed like the ideal time for Israel, with American backing, to make an advantageous deal that would allow it to retain many of the gains resulting from its victory in the 1967 War and yet win public approval by backing a diplomatic approach that promised to resolve the conflict through a mutually acceptable negotiated peace agreement.

In the years that followed, those with views hostile to the Oslo Accords gradually darkened the clouds that have always hung over this peace process. From the Israeli point of view, an upsurge of terrorist incidents, including suicide bombings, made it appear as though the Palestinian side was still committed to violent resistance. Further, was the fact that Arafat was either insincere in his endorsement of the Oslo approach or could not control the behavior of those in the Palestinian camp who refused to accept the legitimacy of an Israeli state. It was also being reported in the West that Arafat sounded more militant when addressing Arab audiences than when talking at the UN or in international venues, and that he was alleged to be doing less than was possible to control the violent activities of the more radical groups in the Palestinian camp. Such interpretations were relied upon to discredit Arafat, and to embolden Israel even to attack his compound and declare him an unfit "partner" for peace talks.

At least as disillusioning from the Palestinian side, was the continued Israeli settlement activity, abetted by an expensive network of settler only roads, that seemed decisively inconsistent with implementing the five-year timetable for Israeli withdrawal from the Palestinian territory occupied in 1967, as was also the case with respect to various moves in Israeli law involving the further consolidation of control over the whole of Jerusalem. Such mixed signals given the postulates of the Oslo Accords were strongly reinforced by the rising strength of the settler-dominated Likud Party, which resulted in Benjamin Netanyahu's first period as prime minister between 1996 and 1999. Netanyahu had been an opponent of Oslo diplomacy from its inception, as well as a proponent of the settlement phenomenon and biblical claims, and this cast further doubts on Israel's commitment to any conception of peace that involved the establishment of a Palestinian state, let alone resolution of the other non-territorial Palestinian grievances. As with Arafat, there were further suspicions aroused because Netanyahu within Israel spoke of the West Bank as "Judea and Samaria," a coded complicity with the Greater Israel forces in the country that formed an important part of his political base, while in international settings he continued to profess faith in direct negotiations and refrained from any public repudiation of the Oslo Accords.

This undermining of the Oslo Accords was hidden from world public opinion as neither side wanted to seem to be "rejectionist" in relation to the two-state solution, a posture that would have angered the United States. It may have been the case that Arafat up to the end of his life continued to believe in the attainability of the core Palestinian goal of statehood. It could be argued that such a diminished conception of Palestinian self-determination was the realistic outer limit of what could be achieved given the power disparities, and that such an outcome was far preferable than enduring the torments of occupation and refugee camps for the indefinite future.

In addition, it remains to this day far easier for the international community to continue to uphold "the peace process" as it was set forth in the Oslo Accords than to acknowledge its breakdown. The United States in particular has continued to act as if this was the only means to resolve the conflict, and that such a course of action is far more politically acceptable than either exerting sufficient pressure on Israel to halt and substantially reverse the settlement process, or acknowledging to the world that conditions no longer favored Palestinian self-determination in the form that had been prefigured in SC Resolution 242 and in subsequent diplomatic commentary. Even if stalled, the Oslo process enabled the West to avoid a direct challenge to Israel without frontally alienating the Arab and Muslim worlds.

The high point of this approach came when Labor was once more briefly in control of the Israeli Government, with Ehud Barack as prime minister. The Last Hurrah of Oslo was the Camp David initiative of Bill Clinton at the very last stage of his presidency in the year 2000. Barack put forward proposals that were described as "generous" in the West, but did not clearly commit Israel to a full withdrawal, nor did it specify what land would be swapped for the territory ceded to Israel so as to enable its incorporation of the so-called "settlement blocs," nor were issues satisfactorily resolved pertaining to refugees, East Jerusalem, or water rights. Some effort was made at the follow-up Taba negotiations in January 2001 to meet several of these Palestinian concerns, but such proposals were not committed to in writing and as reported seemed unlikely to be accepted by the Israel electorate that needed to endorse the agreements in a referendum. These negotiations led to one more diplomatic failure, with Arafat and the PLO cruelly blamed by the United States, despite having been lured to participate against their political will, based on their correct perception that too wide a gap between the minimum demands of the two sides existed to allow negotiations to succeed. The populist Palestinian rejection of the Camp David/Taba outcome resulted in the Second Intifada, which seemed as much directed at the leadership of the PLO for allegedly going along with arrangements that so weakened Palestinian claims as it was against Israel and its policies of occupation and expansion.

Oslo beyond Oslo: The Roadmap and The Quartet

What followed was the presidency of George W. Bush in the United States, and Ariel Sharon in Israel, and a seeming further strengthening of the relationship between the two countries, especially after the 9/11 attacks. Sharon claiming that Arafat was Israel's Osama Bin Laden, and that its security tactics against the Palestinians and the Palestinian leader represented counter-insurgency warfare of the same character as that used by the United States against Al Qaeda. Bush did for the first time clearly indicate that the US conception of a solution to the conflict depended on the establishment of a contiguous Palestinian sovereign state with secure borders and convenient links between Gaza and the West Bank. This result was to be achieved in an incremental process that was renamed The Roadmap, and placed under the auspices of a new framework called The Quartet, consisting of the United States, Russia, the European Union, and the United Nations. Again there were problems with the acceptance of such an approach on both sides. Israel set forth 14 conditions as qualifying its willingness to go along, including its refusal to freeze settlement expansion. There was also no reference made to the protection of Palestinian rights under international law, which seemed to express an intention to resolve the non-territorial dimensions of the conflict (especially, refugees, status of Jerusalem, water resources) by diplomatic bargaining rather than by reference to rights, which implicitly deferred to the power disparities between the parties, which was bad news for the Palestinians.[5]

In this sense, The Roadmap reproduced two of the worst features of the Oslo Accords as text and as existentially evolving process: first, enabling Israel in the course of the occupation to engage in activities unlawful by reference to international humanitarian law, to benefit from the delay in resolving the conflict, and to convert what was clearly unlawful into a new de facto reality that must be taken into account without authorizing challenges prior to the final status negotiations; and second, an unwillingness to allow the Palestinian side to overcome its disadvantages with respect to diplomatic support and power by acknowledging the relevance of international law and Palestinian rights as relevant to the resolution of what were described as "final status" issues, which include settlements, refugees, water, borders, and Jerusalem. In effect, the Oslo Accords, as superseded in negotiating contexts by The Roadmap, have worked out to be a formula for the non-realization of the vision of a sustainable peace between the two sides as projected in general terms by the canonical Security Council Resolution 242. The disconnect between text and de facto circumstances is disguised to this day by continuing to espouse the Resolution 242-plus Oslo-plus Roadmap approach without any formal reference to Israel's actions that have undermined such an outcome as a practical political possibility.

Although the format was adapted to a new phase in the process, The Roadmap approach essentially maintained continuity with Oslo, sustaining the disparity between the two sides, which allowed Israel to assemble more and more facts on the ground, while the clock of the occupation continued to tick. Time was not neutral as between the two sides. Delay was beneficial for Israeli expansionism, and continuously diminished Palestinian hopes and prospects. These facts included the construction of a separation wall mainly on Palestinian territory, appropriating Palestinian land, cutting many Palestinians off from their villages and farmlands in a manner found unlawful in the 2004 Advisory Opinion of the International Court of Justice.[6] It also included the elaborate network of settler-only roads that contributed to the growing apartheid structure of the occupation and made it ever clearer that Israel had no intention of ever completely withdrawing from the West Bank in accord with the plain meaning of Resolution 242.

The United States continued to shield Israel from censure and sanctions, despite its *unlawful* activities that rendered the prospect of a truly sovereign Palestinian state less and less plausible with each passing year, and to dominate the actual diplomatic interaction of the parties. And, of course, the Palestinians were not entirely passive, Hamas firing rockets at southern Israeli towns, which while doing little damage did create fear on the Israeli side of the border with Gaza, and maintained the sort of tension and climate of violence that was incompatible with a politics of reconciliation. There is much controversy over the interactive timeline of violence, determining which side was the provoker and which the retaliator. Further, from Gaza, it was not always clear whether the rockets were being launched with Hamas' approval or by militias that eluded or defied Hamas' control.

The post-1967 occupation continued along the lines set forth in the Oslo Accords, with the territorial administration divided between the Palestinian Authority and Israel, with Israel continuing to maintain several hundred roadblocks throughout the West Bank, which greatly hampered Palestinian mobility, and exercised unrestricted authority to use force in the name of its security. In this respect, Oslo has led to a partially collaborative relationship on security issues as between Israel and the Palestinian Authority, including daily cooperation with

Israeli administrative authorities, and the training of internal security personnel in those parts of the West Bank under Palestinian control being undertaken with American financial assistance and overall involvement. Especially in light of the conflict between the Palestinian Authority and Hamas, particularly after Hamas took control of the Gaza Strip in mid-2007 after a bloody struggle with Fatah, there has been no unified Palestinian representation for diplomatic initiatives. There occurred, in recent years, documented charges of abuse associated both with the PA's policies in the West Bank and Hamas in Gaza toward their respective Palestinian political adversaries. The West Bank and Gaza moved in separate directions, with the West Bank seeking to develop state-like institutions despite the occupation, while Gaza increasingly seemed to go its separate way, increasingly cut-off from the rest of occupied Palestine and enduring an Israeli blockade. Such divisions have further weakened Palestinian diplomatic capacity, a process definitely encouraged by Israel and the United States as expressed by the insistence on treating the elected government of Gaza as "a terrorist organization" rather than as a political actor, an approach reinforced by the comprehensive blockade on exports and imports that has been imposed since 2007, and widely denounced as a flagrant form of collective punishment in direct violation of Article 33 of the 4th Geneva Convention dealing with belligerent occupation.

In 2004, Bush even went to the extreme of an exchange of letters with Sharon, as respective heads of state, agreeing that Israel would have American support for the territorial incorporation of its unspecified large settlement blocs. It was an act of unsurpassed arrogance for an American president to purport to determine that settlements established in violation of international humanitarian law could be transferred to Israeli territorial sovereign control without even seeking Palestinian participation in reaching such a conclusion. Such an assertion also seemed to have been a unilateral modification of the reasonable expectations created by the Oslo Accords and reaffirmed by The Roadmap. It is true that in secret negotiations the Palestinian Authority seemed to accept the substance of what Bush had agreed to, but whether this would be acceptable to the Palestinian people seems doubtful.[7] At the same time, it was Bush who clearly affirmed for the first time that a peaceful solution to the conflict would result in what was promised to be a viable Palestinian state.

Conclusion

The present situation with respect to peace diplomacy is unacceptable. On the Israeli side, there is the offer of unconditional direct negotiations, but with no willingness to suspend, much less halt, the settlement process. On the Palestinian side, as formally represented by the PA and Mahmoud Abbas, is an insistence that such negotiations cannot go forward without a settlement freeze, although not necessarily incorporating settlements in East Jerusalem. Both sides do not question the credibility of the peace process of the sort initially foreshadowed in the Oslo Accords, but greatly undermined in credibility by several intervening developments: the split on the Palestinian side between Fatah and Hamas; the right wing, pro-settler consensus governing Israel, and the expansion of the settlements, the construction of the separation wall, and the deepening of the Jewish presence in East Jerusalem. From these perspectives, the Oslo Accords/Roadmap should be pronounced finally as dead ends so far as peace is concerned.

But there are other issues present. Oslo did accord Palestinian self-government in relation to the majority of the Palestinian urban population in the West Bank, and by the disengagement move of Israel in 2005, a similar result was achieved for the whole of the Gaza Strip. Despite the tribulations of this altered form of occupation, it did allow a certain type of normalcy and autonomy to flourish in both the West Bank and Gaza, and is certainly preferable from the perspective of the Palestinian people, to the type of direct military occupation that existed after the 1967 War and lasted until the partial Israel withdrawal arranged by way of Oslo. The effects of this post-Oslo arrangement is controversial, with many Palestinians contending that it undermined the will to resist by creating complex networks of quasi-dependence of the Palestinian Authority on Israeli financial and political cooperation, and reinforced the disastrous Fatah/Hamas split. From the PA perspective, the road to statehood has been recently advanced by the November 29, 2012 vote in the General Assembly to confer on Palestine the status of "non-member statehood," an outcome surprisingly supported at the last minute even by Hamas. Such a Palestinian state seems valid under international law, but is a far cry even from the Resolution 242 image, which is itself a far cry from the Resolution 181 conception—each iteration of Palestinian statehood was greatly reduced as compared to its predecessor.[8]

At this stage, the sponsors of the Oslo approach, especially the United States and the other members of The Quartet, need either to explain how in view of intervening developments the way forward to the realization of two states for two peoples can be achieved, or acknowledge that the approach is no longer politically attainable, and that the pretension that it is, has become morally unacceptable.

In many respects, Palestinian resistance hopes have shifted to the context of a Legitimacy War, which depends essentially on a soft power global approach. Its current centerpiece is a growing campaign of solidarity with the Palestinian struggle taking the form of BDS: boycott, divestment, and sanctions. This campaign is loosely modeled on the anti-apartheid campaign that was so effective in bringing a largely peaceful end to the racist regime in South Africa. Perhaps, the time has come for civil society at least to switch its hopes and allegiances away from the Oslo/Roadmap approach, and put its efforts solidly behind BDS and the logic of Legitimacy War.

Despite the passage of years, Edward Said's wise words written in 2000 still hold true, and remain as unheeded as ever:

My assumption throughout is that as a Palestinian I believe neither the Arabs nor the Israelis have a real military option, and that the only hope for the future is a decent fair coexistence between the two peoples based upon equality and self-determination.[9]

3
Rethinking the Palestinian Future[1]

Outsiders Speaking for Palestinians

Part of the Palestinian tragedy, ever since the fall of the Ottoman Empire, is that others have again and again presumed to talk on behalf of the Palestinian people. Because of the manner in which the world is organized, these alien voices have consistently overridden Palestinian voices on the basis of geopolitical calculations and Orientalist thinking, to the detriment of the Palestinian people. The roots of this distorting process reached a dramatic climax in the 1917 declaration of Lord Arthur Balfour. His infamous letter to the head of the Zionist movement decreeing that the United Kingdom would look with favor upon the establishment of "a national home for the Jewish people" in historic Palestine signaled a grief-stricken future for the country and the region.

This narrative of colonial "otherness" continued throughout the 30 years of the British Mandate. Its milestone was the 1937 Peel Commission Report, an aggravating imperial initiative that came up with the characteristically British idea that Palestine should be partitioned between Jews and Arabs, putting forward its colonialist endorsement of the Zionist undertaking, without bothering to obtain indigenous consent. The Peel recommendations were significantly embedded in the 1947 United Nations Partition Plan, which assigned 55 percent of Palestinian territory to the Israeli side and 45 percent to the Palestinian side. This allocation defied both the will of the Palestinian population and the demographic balance in Palestine, which at the time had a greater than two-thirds Arab majority. This neo-colonial approach to Palestine has been sustained since Israel proclaimed itself a sovereign state. Acting precipitously, the UN admitted Israel as a member without a sufficient *prior* effort to secure Palestinian rights under international law or the consent of the indigenous population.

Thus, at the very historical moment that colonized communities and peoples were discrediting European colonialism and defeating it in wars of liberation around the world, Britain was consigning Palestine to a new variant of European settler-colonialism, a catastrophic process for the Palestinian people. The *nakba* of 1948, which featured massive dispossession of Palestinians and the destruction of more than 600 Palestinian villages, was followed by a second cycle of dispossession in 1967 that resulted in the prolonged occupation and partial de facto annexation of the Palestinian territorial remnant. Nor has the 1967 occupation been static: it has been used by the Israelis ever since to realize their vision of "Greater Israel." Israel's efforts to control the West Bank and Jerusalem have been relentless, relying on a combination of annexation, manipulation of residency and building permits, the establishment and continuous expansion of settlements, and coercive demographics.

External support both for the denial of Palestinian self-determination and for Israeli expansionism has been a consistent feature of the almost 70 years of Israel's existence as an independent state. Its de facto borders as proposed by the UN were extended by force of arms during the 1948 war, increasing Israel's share of historic Palestine from the UN-proposed 55 percent to the 78 percent possessed when an armistice agreement was finally reached. After the 1967 war, the expanded borders (and the expanded territory they encompassed) were given implicit and provisional de jure recognition by the UN Security Council in canonical Resolution 242. These were the borders to which the PLO subsequently acquiesced in the historic concessions of its 1988 declaration of Palestinian independence, which in essence recognized and accepted Israel's permanent existence. Some years later, these borders were also accepted de facto by the Arab states by virtue of their 2002 peace initiative as well as by several American presidents—in the latter case with additional elements in Israel's favor, including support for Israel's retention of settlement blocs, recognition of Israel's security concerns in the Jordan Valley, and so-called "land swaps" that would reset the 1967 borders.

Even here, then, it is mainly outsiders who are pronouncing upon what is fair and reasonable for the two peoples in a distorted manner that reflects Zionist influence in shaping US, European, and even UN diplomacy. The point here is that the Palestinian ordeal has been operationalized at every stage by the weight of alien political forces not genuinely supportive of the inalienable Palestinian right of self-determination. As the most fundamental of human rights, self-determination has been set forth as the common Article 1 in the two foundational documents depicting political legitimacy since the end of World War II: the two Human Rights Covenants of 1966.

The USA as an Honest Broker

In some respects, the most insidious of the outside voices is that of the US government, which purports to be capable of simultaneously performing three incompatible functions: providing its diplomatic good offices as an "honest broker"; pronouncing authoritatively upon the contours of a fair solution; and repeatedly demonstrating (and profusely reaffirming) its abiding, unshakeable pro-Israeli partisanship. Washington's willingness to differ publicly with Israel was tested when President Obama in his first years in office reaffirmed the 1967 borders as the basis for direct negotiations, seeming to suggest a modest US effort to rehabilitate its claim to be an "honest broker," but this gesture of balance was not sustained, and such opinions were never repeated.

We can all speculate as to why the Palestinian Authority does not scream in dismay at being expected to fall in line with American diplomatic initiatives that are in effect cleared with the Israeli government at every stage. Rashid Khalidi's devastating critique of US Middle East policy in his convincing book, transparently titled *Brokers of Deceit: How the US has Undermined Peace in the Middle East*, is relevant in this regard. Its most starkly illuminating finding is that there has never been any serious deviation from the course set by Menachem Begin at the Camp David negotiations in 1978, when he proclaimed that "'under no condition' can a Palestinian state be created."[2] Even Yitzhak Rabin is conclusively shown to have remained inalterably opposed to the emergence of a genuinely sovereign Palestinian state. Such a well-documented finding is devastating because it discloses the abyss between Israeli (and more importantly US) public diplomacy, which posits the two-state solution as an agreed outcome of negotiations, and the awareness that Israel's leaders have been privately committed all along to avoiding such a solution. This outcome has been elaborately

24

confirmed in Jeremy Hammond's *Obstacle to Peace*, which if fairly heeded would put an end to this double coding of American diplomacy pertaining to the Palestinian national struggle.[3]

In his 2013 visit to Israel, President Obama abandoned his earlier show of impartiality in an undisguised effort to overcome the hostility of the Netanyahu leadership in Tel Aviv, which had made no secret of backing Mitt Romney in the 2012 US presidential elections. While Obama could have seized the occasion of his re-election to adopt a more independent approach to the conflict and try to attain credibility as, at least, a semi-honest broker, he chose to go in the opposite direction, perhaps tactically with his domestic priorities in the United States uppermost in his thinking.

After lauding Israel in every conceivable manner in his Jerusalem speech of March 21, 2013, including a gratuitous pledge to further augment US military support, Obama praised Israel's past efforts to find peace with the Palestinians, expressing understanding at the frustrations that have led many Israelis to be "skeptical" as to whether peace "can be achieved."[4] He even deferred to Israel's ultimate right to decide what it is prepared to do to reach a resolution of the conflict: "I know that only Israelis can make the fundamental decisions about your country's future."[5] Obama exhibited no comparable sensitivity to Palestinian ultimate and inalienable rights to decide upon their future, which is a rather demeaning oversight considering that Palestinians, unlike the Israelis, have been living as refugees, in exile, under occupation since 1967, and as a subjugated minority since 1948.

Obama went on to restate conventional wisdom about the end goal of diplomacy by asserting that "the only way for Israel to endure and thrive as a Jewish and democratic state is through the realization of an independent and viable Palestine."[6] Yet he gave no indication during the entire speech about what might be necessary to make this goal attainable under present conditions. He never broached the subject of what could be done to shrink the unlawful archipelago of Israeli settlements in the West Bank; or to end ethnic manipulations in occupied Jerusalem; or to dismantle the separation wall declared illegal in 2004 by a virtually unanimous International Court of Justice; or voicing a bit of skepticism about the political make-up of the extremist Netanyahu cabinet, which is even more pro-settler, more pro-annexationist, and more generally belligerent than any of its predecessors. And with no reference to the unpromising context in which to attempt a resumption of the peace process, Obama blandly encouraged the renewal of direct negotiations between Tel Aviv and Ramallah, without even proposing prior "confidence-building measures" that could give needed credibility to his advocacy.

Obama's call seemed a naive repetition of what had been put forward during the Bush-II presidency by invoking the outworn formula of "two states for two peoples." To my ears, the Obama administration's invocation of the two-state mantra sounded at the time like a surrealistic evasion of a far more discouraging reality. It amounts to a cynical sting operation directed at the Palestinians. Its ulterior motive would seem to be to revalidate the Israeli occupation by showing Israeli good faith in resuming negotiations and Palestinian rejectionism in resisting them, or suffering through another round of fruitless negotiations. Or, maybe a Plan B was to induce the Palestinian Authority to accept a non-viable Palestinian statelet, which Netanyahu, Obama, and maybe even Abbas would proclaim as finally fulfilling the agreed goal of two states for two peoples. This could even be memorialized by a second handshake on the White House lawn, or even a second Nobel Peace Prize.

The Problem of Representation

It may be worth recalling that the federal government of the United States deceived the Native Americans over and over again, leading them to renounce their rights in one-sided treaty negotiations. The Palestinian people should take heed from this history and exercise the greatest caution before relinquishing their rights under international law when pressured to accept arrangements reflecting "facts on the ground" as the best deal possible. It should be understood that the hard power imbalances of the present are oblivious to the tenets of international law and insensitive to the minimal content of twenty-first-century global justice.

Unless a fundamental but improbable shift occurs in Israeli thinking, Israel and the United States never will (as they never have), genuinely accept the idea of a fully sovereign state of Palestine. Despite lip service to the contrary, Israel does not accept the supposed global consensus that eventually emerged from Security Council Resolution 242 calling for Israel's withdrawal from the territory it seized in the 1967 War—

that is, that a sovereign Palestinian state should be established within the 1967 borders. Even this vague and ambiguous miniaturization of the Palestinian right of self-determination (limited, at most, to 22 percent of the territory administered the British Mandate) was never clearly accepted by Israel's leadership, irrespective of the party in power. Nor did Washington ever question this cardinal feature of Israeli rejectionism, in part undoubtedly because US comprehension of the conflict was shaped by such top advisors as Dennis Ross and Martin Indyk without even the creative friction that might have been provided by the participation of less partisan viewpoints. These bureaucratic insiders approached management of the so-called peace process with the uncontested imprimatur of impeccable American Israel Public Affairs Committee (AIPAC)[7] credentials.

American intervention in Israel's favor extends to intra-Palestinian politics as well, such as the exclusion and demonization of Hamas. As already noted, Hamas has governed the Gaza Strip alone since mid-2007 after it emerged the winner in a struggle with Fatah's US-backed military challenge to the Hamas-led Gaza government—a government that had resulted from Hamas's electoral victory the previous year. Since the Hamas–Fatah split, intermittent unity talks between the Palestinian Authority and Hamas, based on the pragmatics of reconciliation, have been held but so far have only produced weak arrangements that quickly fell apart. These unity efforts have been consistently opposed by both Tel Aviv and Washington. To some extent, the Palestinians' failure to mend fences is due to Israeli and US warnings that adverse consequences would follow from the formation of any political arrangement that includes Hamas in the representation of Palestine. Hamas remains blacklisted as "a terrorist organization" and will doubtless remain so until a moment arrives when Israel and the United States seek a peaceful end to the conflict.

This remains a harmful feature of the Palestinian diplomatic position. All Palestinian constituencies at this point recognize the desirability of a unified leadership that could articulate Palestinian grievances, demands, and rights in the course of negotiations. Reports that the Palestinian Authority maintains a willingness to resume direct negotiations with Israel without any provision for the inclusion of Hamas casts further doubt on whether the Palestinian people are currently being represented in an acceptable manner.

The only condition that the Palestinian Authority has put forward is a demand that settlement expansion in the West Bank be suspended during negotiations.

These considerations do not even take into account the representation of Palestinian refugees and exiles, constituencies estimated to total 7 million, which makes them a majority among the Palestinian people. This is yet another aspect of Palestinian representation that further complicates the task of identifying which Palestinian voice(s) at this time can legitimately and authoritatively speak for the Palestinian people as a whole in the pursuit of their collective goals. This matter of representation cannot be resolved altogether by formalities and legalisms. Given the widespread perception of a quasi-collaborative and subordinated relationship with Israel and the United States, can the Palestinian Authority and the PLO act as the authentic and inclusive voices representing Palestinians in foreign refugee camps and living in countries throughout the world? For all of the reasons identified above, to speculate about the future is to walk upon treacherous terrain.

A Note on Solidarity

My own understanding of where we are as a species is such that I believe it imperative that we consider ourselves, first and foremost, as members of the human family, and only secondarily as belonging to this or that ethnicity, nationality, gender, religion, or tribe. This affirmation of human identity remains a rather empty vessel unless it is enriched by readiness to listen to "the other," especially to those others who live at the margins due to poverty, alternative sexuality, minority status, persecution, and so on. There is, then, what might be called "a politics of identity" that has two aspects: an affirmative species identity, and a capacity to listen to the grievances of those who endure deprivations because of who they are, or put differently, to the sub-species category with which they identify.

Yet I would not advocate such a cosmopolitan position for those who are enduring severe deprivations. Thus, when it comes to the Palestinians, and other peoples in the Global South, who are daily confronting alien and imperial structures of oppression and exploitation, their sense of self is understandably focused on their primary most immediate, and long stressed, identity and aspirations. In oppressive circumstances, emancipation comes before human solidarity.

For myself, having lived all my life on the American side of the global divide between West and non-West, I can base my moral engagement as a human being on taking the suffering of others seriously. Indeed, I have come to view this as the defining commitment of a political culture that is genuinely dedicated to the realization of human rights. For a variety of personal and intellectual reasons, this understanding has led me over the years to identify more and more closely with the Palestinian struggle. Three decades earlier, a similar outlook led me to feel solidarity with the Vietnamese struggle in their anti-colonial wars, first against France and then against the American government. Later, to a lesser extent but still relevant, I felt this same solidarity with the global anti-apartheid campaign and the civil rights movement in the United States.

Of course, solidarity does not mean a total suspension of disbelief. Those engaged in this struggle, whether Palestinian or not, whether living under occupation or not, have their own ethical compasses by which to guide their judgments and behavior. Solidarity does not mean endorsing suicide bombing, and does not require approving of violent forms of resistance that target civilians or vigilante executions of suspected collaborators. But nor does it necessarily mean the automatic condemnation of all violent tactics of resistance. The Israeli journalists Amira Hass's and Gideon Levy's sympathetic commentaries on Palestinian stone-throwing at Israel Defense Forces (IDF) soldiers and their tanks are illuminating and ethically important.[8] They express the dual metaphorical sense that stone-throwing by those living under occupation is both a metaphor for resistance and a meaningful, substantive expression of a will to resist. This is especially valid when the resistors are people long oppressed, completely outgunned, and denied any reasonable means to exercise their rights of self-defense, and when it applies to an occupation that has for decades massively and callously violated the fundamental norms of international humanitarian law.

Given Israel's disproportionate responses and punitive policies, stone-throwing is, along with the recent hunger strikes among Palestinian prisoners, the most compelling expression of that seminal Palestinian cultural virtue, *sumud* (steadfastness). Stone-throwing also dramatizes the disparity between the occupying power's ultra-modern military capabilities and the dependence of an occupied people on resisting by the only means available to them, the stones on the ground. This disparity shows up in any comparison, including tellingly in the level of casualties experienced by the two sides.

In essence, there are solidarity perspectives that reflect moral assessments (for example, refusal to target civilians) and there are perspectives that defer to the judgment of those who are being directly victimized. Both are valid, but even outsiders are responsible for deciding for themselves what is permissible and what is not. Against this background of disclaimers, I will share my understanding of the present situation and its future implications, not by pretending to be above the fray, but as a friend of the Palestinian people and their long struggle for their rights and for peace with dignity.

Renewing the Palestinian Quest

Thirty-five years ago, in a section of his book *The Question of Palestine* titled "Uncertain Future," Edward Said wrote, "Two things are certain: the Jews of Israel will remain, the Palestinians will also remain. To say much more than this with assurance is foolish."[9] This assertion remains central to our understanding of what is possible and currently desirable in two crucial respects. First, any assertion beyond the minimal fact that both peoples will remain present in the contested territory is still impossible to make with the slightest confidence. Thus the future for both peoples is beclouded by uncertainties. Second, the relative position of the Palestinians has deteriorated far beyond what Said lamented so eloquently when his book was published in 1979.

At present, one can do little more than take note of an altered approach by the Palestinians to the ongoing struggle that places its emphasis on nonviolent tactics of resistance, and de-emphasizes, at least for now, reliance on armed resistance. The new approach involves the character of which I have in the past called a "Legitimacy War," a major dimension of which involves support for global solidarity campaigns that are in harmony with and expressions of authentic Palestinian aspirations. As suggested, the issue of what is "authentic" is itself a contested discourse within the wider Palestinian community, and cannot be taken for granted.

In speculating about the future, I am consciously privileging a "politics of emancipation," (gaining freedom from structures of oppression, which in the Palestinian case means not only the occupation, but the reversible effects of forcible dispossession) either in its primal form of the Palestinian people or in its derivative form of solidarity with the Palestinian people. What this also reflects is an understanding of global justice that initially gives priority to overcoming instances of acute injustice. There is embedded here a time dimension that pertains to the Palestinian experience of dispossession and injustice that shapes the scope of demands and expectations for the Palestinians. If the major grievance is connected with the Balfour Declaration, it is quite different from accepting the developments on the ground as of 1948 or 1967. The contention that Palestinians should allow Israel to incorporate the settlement blocs is an indirect way of imposing a timeline that is fixed by *present* realities. It is important to ask: "Where should the origins of the relevant timeline be situated?" from the perspective of asserting at the present moment the content of the Palestinian claim of self-determination. As suggested, there are several alternative ways to put forward Palestinian claims based on how the narrative of the conflict is conceptualized for diplomatic purposes. Each of the foundational moments identified above can be supported from either principled or pragmatic standpoints, and at some point, it is the responsibility of the legitimate representatives of the Palestinian people to make such a choice, which is bound to be controversial among Palestinians, especially if disunity persists.

Posing such an issue brings to light several interconnected issues: how to balance the quest for justice against the goals of a secure peace and a humane governing process at the earliest possible time? In seeking a definition of a just outcome of the Palestinian struggle, what account should be taken of Israeli counter-narratives? Given the discouraging configuration of present realities, I am seeking to grasp more clearly how to articulate Palestinian goals. I am striving for a sense of how Palestinian "emancipation" might best be understood at this point in history, and how tempered it must be by realistic constraints and empathy for "the Israeli other," by the realities of the past century, and by rights as conferred by international law.

Resorting to a terminology I have used in other settings, what is the relevant "horizon of feasibility" as compared to the "horizon of necessity" and the "horizon of desire"? How do we seek an outcome that best walks the tightrope between fulfilling Palestinian claims under international law and accepting the reality of an Israeli state, within the 1967 borders—one whose presence seemed to have been accepted as a reality by the UN (in 1967), the PLO (in 1988), and the Arab states (in 2002)? Can we identify some "horizons of necessity" in a political space where the most compelling Palestinian grievances can be addressed without undermining the basic identity of Israeli society? Perhaps by posing this dual objective, I am calling attention to its implausibility, especially from the perspective of the 20 percent Palestinian minority inside Israel, which has been enduring multiple forms of discrimination ever since the establishment of the state in 1948.

The Palestinian minority in Israel have lived as second-class citizens and as targets of Zionist purists actively seeking either to have them expelled, or to have their population centers administratively transferred to fall under the jurisdiction of Ramallah. Who now represents this Palestinian minority living in Israel? The so-called peace process that has dominated diplomacy since the 1993 Oslo framework is centered around a land-for-peace formula that completely erases this substantial segment of the Palestinian people from the political consciousness of those engaged in periodic negotiations. The same dynamic of erasure, although somewhat less totally, applies to the several million Palestinian refugees who claim an organic connection between just treatment for themselves and a sustainable and just peace.

If abstracted from the historical context, there is something manifestly unjust about granting a right of return to a Jew whose family has lived for generations in an American city while denying this right to a Palestinian who was forced to flee the village in which his ancestors lived from time immemorial, but which is now located in Israel. In effect, is Zionist Israel—which insists on being treated, even by its Palestinian citizens, as a Jewish state—compatible with the most fundamental precepts of human dignity? Has it become unsustainable in a globalizing world where peoples of diverse backgrounds inevitably intermingle? Can a state be legitimate in the twenty-first century if it does not treat those subject to its authority with total equality, if it instead claims for itself the prerogative to privilege a particular ethnicity or religion and subordinate all others? Certainly, inequalities will arise due to demographic and socio-economic imbalances that give greater weight and benefits to some identities than to others. But what seems to have become unacceptable over the last century is endowing inequalities with a de jure status. The combination of human rights and globalization underscores the importance of legitimating only such governing processes as rest on principles of inconclusiveness.

Horizons of Feasibility

Let us first consider the Palestinian future from the perspective of horizons of feasibility, which focuses on what politicians deem attainable given the constraints. Such horizons reflect the prevailing *rhetorical* consensus among the respective government elites in Tel Aviv, Washington, and Ramallah. On a substantive basis, the horizon of feasibility considers both the nature of the Israeli state and any questioning of territorial Zionism to be politically unacceptable and beyond responsible debate. On a procedural basis, the uniform call is for a resumption of direct negotiations of the sort that have periodically taken place ever since the adoption of the Oslo framework three decades ago.

From everything we know of the present Netanyahu government— its undisguised settlement expansion plans and opposition to the creation of a viable Palestinian state, its total rejection of any right of return for Palestinian refugees and their descendants, etc—there is no reason to suppose that any progress whatsoever can be achieved toward reaching a diplomatic solution that is fair to the Palestinians. The current Israeli leadership is the direct heir of Ze'ev Jabotinsky's "iron wall"[10] or Revisionist variant of Zionism. The Revisionists held, inter alia, that a Jewish state required the expulsion or subjugation of the native population and that no division of the land or its control could be accepted.

Jabotinsky also believed negotiations over territory would be futile, since the Palestinians would oppose their dispossession from their ancestral land with every means at their disposal. Even David Ben-Gurion, Israel's founder and the supposed soul of moderate and progressive Zionism, was clear that the struggle was one of survival, either "us" or "them." On this matter he essentially agreed with his arch-rival, albeit in private or as manifested through his actions. "If

I was an Arab leader," he once confided to Nahum Goldmann, "I would not make terms with Israel. That is natural: we have taken their country. They only see one thing: we have come here and stolen their country. Why should they accept that?"[11] Ben-Gurion's words remain relevant, and should be reflected upon by all those whose thoughts and feelings would make them want to respond to horizons of feasibility. Zionism at its heart is about maximizing territory of the land of biblical Israel, not about finding formulas for mutually acceptable coexistence on the land.

Only by grasping this Zionist consensus on the nature and scope of the struggle can we hope to understand that what has purported to be feasible has actually been unfeasible all along. The horizon of feasibility has served to confuse and cloud accurate perceptions of what is required to end this struggle in a just and sustainable manner. Such confusion has enabled Israel over the decades to extend its grip on almost the entirety of mandate Palestine. This same confusion has also made it possible to engage the Palestinians in the negotiations process while simultaneously downgrading and disregarding their hopes and expectations, however minimally expressed. Time has been against the Palestinian people, and continues to be.

The Palestinian negotiators are not unaware of Israel's unconditional opposition to Palestinian self-determination any more than they are unaware of Israeli thinking about the disposition of territory. The leaked reports of the secret discussions in Jordan between Israeli and Palestinian Authority (PA) representatives make this clear. According to the reports, Israel at the start of the discussions insisted that the Palestinians drop as fruitless any call for withdrawal to the 1967 borders, and urged instead that both sides focus on their distinct interests, taking full account of the realities of the situation on the ground. More concretely, this meant that the PA had to recognize and acquiesce in Israel's interest in finalizing the incorporation of settlements and land behind the separation wall that had been declared illegal by the 2004 World Court advisory opinion. In exchange, the PA interest in having some kind of self-governing political community with a recognized, although qualified, international status would be satisfied. The PA would be free to call it a state, and to put forward indirectly a claim to sovereignty by exploring the possibility of becoming a federal entity that could be integrated into the present state of Jordan. Although the

PA indicated its unwillingness to consider such a game plan as a basis for the renewal of formal negotiations, yet Obama during his 2013 visit to Ramallah still implored the Palestinians to return to the negotiating table without preconditions. One can only wonder, "to what end?"

In sum, horizons of feasibility limit Palestinian options to two: either agree to a further round of negotiations all but certain to fail; or refuse such negotiations and be blamed by Israel, the United States, and mainstream media. The first option would quiet critical public opinion while Israel continues to expand settlements and to further consolidate its hold on East Jerusalem and would likely leave the PA to bear most of the blame in the world media while also being subjected to Palestinian anger and disgust for even agreeing to take part in such a futile enterprise. The second option—refusing negotiations—would feed Israel's propaganda that it has no choice, absent a Palestinian partner for peace, but to proceed unilaterally with its national policies. On the other hand, at least the second option would not implicate the PA in a self-defeating diplomatic charade, and would lay the ground for a clearer perception of the Israeli game plan, a central plank of which is denial of fundamental Palestinian rights.

Horizons of Necessity and Desire

Horizons of necessity are premised on the idea that a sustainable and just peace is an urgent imperative following from the recognition that present circumstances impose unacceptable burdens on the Palestinian people that have been endured for too long, and should be ended forthwith. This is not a prediction of what will happen, but a statement of moral necessity. From a predictive standpoint, no end is in sight with regard to a just and sustainable peace. Horizons of necessity and desire fail to redress historic grievances associated with the initial establishment of a Jewish homeland. They accept the irreversibility of the homeland claim while affirming the Palestinian need for (and entitlement to) a viable state of their own. For the Israelis, necessity in the context of peace cannot be allowed to mean less than a secure Israel within the 1967 borders. For the Palestinians, it must entail transforming the present situation into one where Palestinian self-determination could be achieved in a manner consistent with Palestinians and Israelis either living side by side (in separate states), or together in a just and likely sustainable manner within a single state. The side-by-side solution requires the removal of all laws and practices that discriminate against the Palestinian minority in Israel, and would presuppose the realization of Palestinian rights under international law (including for refugees) and an Israeli withdrawal to the 1967 borders (with only minor modifications), as well as the dismantlement of the separation wall and most settlements. According to my political compass, such an outcome, though morally and legally expressive of a minimum embodiment of Palestine's right of self-determination, is not attainable for the foreseeable future.

Equally unattainable, but potentially capable of fulfilling the requirements of necessity (or at least of identifying a solution *based* on horizons of necessity) would be a single secular state for Jews and Palestinians within the same boundaries as Mandatory Palestine. This single-state alternative could be operationalized without substantially altering the situation on the ground. In principle, it would treat Israelis and Palestinians equally in all respects and would base rights on citizenship rather than ethnicity. It would not require either a massive denial of equality for the Palestinians or require the Israelis to make huge adjustments in the distribution of the Jewish population within the country, though it may require regulating immigration policy into something fair between ethnicities and religions.

From my perspective, this single, democratic, secular state, based on equal rights for all those resident in the country, is the outcome that most accords with *horizons of desire*. If such an image of living together could be converted into a political project, horizons of desire could become the means to overcome the present gap between feasibility and necessity. Of course, realistically, this one-state variant on Palestinian self-determination is not feasible in the current political atmosphere, since it would mean the end of Zionism as presently understood as it would require Israel to abandon or drastically modify the exclusivist features of Zionist ideology, and be content with a homeland rather than an ethnocracy.

It is possible to imagine other positive solutions with a better chance of meeting the horizons of necessity, such as an arrangement that would involve a wider confederation of peoples by including neighboring countries—a solution that could reduce tensions that have accumulated for over a century between Jewish settlers and the Palestinian indigenous population.

In general, however, are horizons of desire to be considered utopian? Of course they are. Yet the feasibility alternative alone is dystopian. I believe that only horizons of desire can create confidence in the Palestinian future, and that it is up to Palestinians to embrace whatever image of "desire" they wish to affirm.

Freeing the Political and Moral Imagination

In effect, we need to free the political and moral imagination from the dead end characteristics of feasibility, acknowledge the necessities of a just peace with dignity, and by so doing, set our sights high above horizons of desire. This is the message that is sent by many Palestinian political prisoners who have been resisting Israeli occupation for decades. This is the message of Palestine's poet, Mahmoud Darwish, it is the message of Edward Said, and it is the message that I wish to impart by way of invoking these inspirational Palestinian voices. This is also the message of the "Legitimacy War" being waged by Palestine on many symbolic and substantive battlefields throughout the world to gain control of the legal and moral heights, and thereby strengthen the legitimacy of Palestinian claims.

There exists an implicit message of hope at the heart of the Boycott, Divestment, and Sanctions campaign (BDS), which is building a global solidarity movement based on nonviolent coercion, and gains confidence from the outcome of many prior anti-colonial struggles and from the success of the worldwide anti-apartheid movement that resulted in the collapse of a racist regime in South Africa. BDS is essentially a secular faith-based movement that seeks to make Israel and the United States rethink and recalculate their sense of "the feasible" in light of the mounting costs and dangers associated with continuing the denial of fundamental Palestinian rights.

4

The Emergent
Palestinian Imaginary

Preliminary Remark

It is often overlooked that as early as 1988, and possibly earlier, the unified Palestinian leadership has decisively opted for what I would call a "sacrificial" peace. By sacrificial, I mean an acceptance of peace and normalization with Israel that is premised upon the surrender of significant Palestinian rights under international law. The contours of this image of a resolved conflict consist of two principal elements: a Palestinian sovereign state within the 1967 "Green Line" borders and a just resolution of the refugee problem. This conception of a durable peace is essentially an application of Security Council Resolutions 242 and 338, and is the foundation of the initiative formally endorsed by the Palestine National Council in 1988.

It is sacrificial in both dimensions of what was declared in advance to be acceptable: a territorial delimitation that was less than half of what the UN partition plan had offered in 1947 by way of the General Assembly Resolution 181, which was reasonable for the Palestinian leadership to reject at the time as well as by the neighboring Arab governments on the grounds that it was imposed in defiance of the will of the Palestinian people and offered the Jewish residents of Palestine 55 percent of the territory even though its land ownership was only 6 percent of the total (and its population share estimated to be 31–33 percent of the total). In effect, the Palestinian acceptance of the 1967 borders overlooked the unlawful acquisition by Israel of territory by forcible means in the 1948 War. It also seemed to signal a readiness to negotiate a solution for the dispossessed Palestinians that fell short of the right of return affirmed by the General Assembly in Resolution 194. From an international law or global justice perspective, it can be argued that the rights of the Palestinian people were severely violated in 1917 by the Balfour Declaration promising a Jewish homeland in Palestine to the Zionist Movement without the slightest effort to consult the people then living in Palestine and by the British administrative policies throughout the mandatory period that favored Jewish immigration and Zionist objectives. It would seem that the full implementation of the Palestinian right of self-determination would involve a questioning of these colonialist origins of the state of Israel. For political and prudential reasons, and in view of the acceptance of Israel as a member of the United Nations, these legal and moral arguments have never been officially insisted upon in Palestinian diplomacy. Also ignored, are the rights of the Palestinian minority of 20 percent, amounting to more than 1.7 million, living within pre-1967 Israel, that have not received equal treatment, nor had their human dignity respected, especially to the extent that Israel not only grants Jews throughout the world an unlimited *right of return* but also insists on being "a Jewish state," what the influential Jewish civic leader in the United States, Henry Siegman, has labeled "an ethnocracy," and no longer credible when claiming to be "a democratic state."[1]

The Arab Peace Initiative of 2002 reaffirms this regional acceptance of such a solution, and the Palestinian Authority in recent years has exhibited a willingness to compromise still further in relation to the Israeli settlement blocs and even foregoing the prospect of having the capital of Palestine in East Jerusalem. Israel on its side has never clearly signaled a similar readiness to establish peace on a sustainable basis that included an acknowledgement of Palestinian *rights*, despite the strong indications that such a solution would produce enhanced *security* for the state of Israel, which is always invoked as the primary demand by the governing authorities in Tel Aviv. In effect, over the years, by a series of interlinked policies, especially the settlement movement, the separation wall, and the annexation and enlargement of the city of Jerusalem, Israel has been unwilling to reach peace on the basis of the 1988 Palestinian offer, and enlarged its minimum security demands to include a variety of strategic and national goals. These extravagant security demands have continuously escalated and are reinforced by occupation policies that are in violation of the Fourth Geneva Convention that sets forth the minimal requirements of international humanitarian law. In defiance, Israel imposes apartheid structures of administration, illegal interferences with Palestinian mobility via checkpoints and closures, engages in ethnic cleansing in East Jerusalem, performs house demolitions throughout Occupied Territories, and uses various techniques to subvert Palestinian residence rights.

It is notable and revealing that neither Israel, nor the United States, have ever even acknowledged this unilateral expression of willingness on the part of Palestine to accept peace on terms that fall far short of the legal and moral entitlements of international law. What is more, there have never been direct or indirect Israeli moves that could qualify as reciprocal gestures. Instead, Israel has persisted with its relentless establishment of "facts on the ground" in violation of international humanitarian law, and has even persuaded the United States, most formally in the 2004 exchange of letters between Ariel Sharon and George W. Bush to accept the core of these facts as establishing a new baseline favorable to Israel for devising a formula to fulfill the promise of "land for peace."

Overall, it is best to view this background as constituted by Israel's continuous inflation of *security* expectations to be realized by the steady diminution of Palestinian *rights*. In effect, the *nakba* associated with the dispossession and dispersal of Palestinians in 1948 should be regarded as a *process* and not just a catastrophic event. Such a national trauma as has been inflicted on the Palestinian people over such a long interval is unprecedented during this historical era of decolonization and the privileging of the right of self-determination.

Three Palestinian Disillusionments

For the more than 65 years that Palestinian hopes and expectation have languished, there have been many efforts by the Palestinian people to constitute, sustain, and build a national movement with the capacity to achieve liberation and realize fundamental Palestinian rights. The present period is one in which there is a clear effort to find a viable post-Oslo strategy and vision that will help restore Palestinian collective identity, which has been shattered ever since the Oslo framework was adopted in 1993, as re-inscribed on the international agenda as The Roadmap of The Quartet on April 30, 2003. The consensus among Palestinians that the Oslo approach is dead continues to be ignored by governmental actors, above all by the United States, which successfully pushed for the resumption of direct negotiations between the government of Israel and the Palestinian Authority that commenced in 2013 and proceeded fitfully until their breakdown in frustration in the Spring, 2014. In contrast, undertaking a reformulation of the Palestinian national movement proceeds independently of world public opinion, and reflects the experience of three disillusionments:

1. *International Law and the Authority of the United Nations*
Especially in the early years after the end of the 1948 War, Palestinians placed their main hopes on the authority of international law, and the support that their struggle seemed to gain at the United Nations, especially in the General Assembly. This support remains important in identifying the contours of a just and sustainable outcome, which needs to reflect a balancing of *rights* rather than a bargaining mechanism as promoted by Oslo and The Quartet that depends on a balancing of *power*, including the treatment of (unlawful) "facts on the ground." The disillusionment arises because having international law on the side of Palestinian grievances relating to occupation policies, borders, Jerusalem, refugees, water, and settlements has not produced results on the level of *practice*. On the contrary, despite the backing of international law and the organized international society, the position of Palestine in relation to overcoming their grievances has continuously deteriorated, especially with respect to the underlying goal of the Palestinian exercise of an inalienable right of self-determination.

2. *Armed Struggle and Wars of Liberation*
The Palestinian national movement, despite its current fragmentation, has for the past seven years or so become generally disillusioned with reliance upon armed struggle as the basis for attaining primary goals of an emancipatory character. Such an abandonment has not involved a principled shift to a politics of nonviolence. Palestine continues to claim the prerogative of relying on force for defensive purposes, as when Israel launches an attack on Gaza or settlers violently attack Palestinians in the West Bank. As Nelson Mandela made so clear in the South African struggle against apartheid, the commitment to nonviolent forms of resistance to an oppressive order does not cancel the right of an oppressed people to use

whatever instruments they find useful, including violence, although limited by an ethos of unconditional respect for civilian innocence. Most of the anti-colonial struggles, legitimated as "wars of national liberation," relied on violence, but achieved their eventual victories mainly through an effective reliance on soft power techniques of social mobilization and the unconditional commitment to sustained opposition by popular forces. In effect, this disillusionment is related with an appreciation that recent historical transformations of an emancipatory kind have most often happened as a result of "people power" rather than through reliance on superior "hard power." This historical interpretation of recent trends in relation to conflict has profound tactical and strategic implications for the Palestinian struggle.

3. *Traditional Diplomacy*

The learning experience for those supporters of the Palestinian struggle of the last 20 years is that inter-governmental diplomacy is not *currently* a pathway to a just peace, but rather a sinkhole for Palestinian rights. The Oslo/Quartet process has facilitated Israeli expansionist designs, confiscating land, building and expanding settlements, and changing the demographics of the occupation, especially in East Jerusalem. Periodic breakdowns of this diplomatic charade helps the Israelis realize their goals at the expense of Palestinian prospects. Time is not neutral under these circumstances, and the long period of gridlock has lowered Palestinian expectations, at least as these are articulated by its formal representatives in Ramallah. From its outset, the diplomacy of the peace process was one-sided and flawed, fragmenting the Palestinian remnant of historic Palestine into areas A, B, and C, relying on the United States as the intermediary despite its undisguised alignment behind Israel and being deeply responsive to Israel's security claims which were continuously inflated while ignoring Palestinian grievances and claims based on international law, and not even mentioning the right of self-determination.

Those who insist on special "security" arrangements usually fear losing what is possessed, while those who call for "rights" are normally seeking what is their entitlement conceived against a background of deprivation and dispossession. From a Palestinian perspective, the framework and process has been thoroughly biased in Israel's favor, and substantive promises have gone unfulfilled. Despite these Palestinian disappointments, due almost entirely to Israel's behavior, it is the Palestinians who are given the lion's share of the blame when the diplomatic negotiations break down periodically.

This disillusionment means that the Palestinian outlook should be by now clearly post-Oslo, that is, what to do given the failure of direct negotiations to produce positive results. This contrasts with the inter-governmental consensus of the United States, Israel, and the Palestinian Authority that insists that such diplomacy is the *only* road to peace despite its record of failure. This spirit of "Oslo is dead, long live Oslo" is clearly defeatist, and manifests the deficiencies of Palestinian representation via Ramallah.

Israel's Strategic Posture and Regional Developments

In part, Palestinian disillusionment has been prompted by Israel's hard power dominance recently reinforced by political developments in the Middle East. To the extent that such disillusionment is interpreted in a defeatist spirit, it ignores Palestinian opportunities to pursue a soft power approach to realize self-determination and other rights so long denied. In effect, interpreting the conflict from a hard power perspective is to base analysis on a false political consciousness given recent historical trends, and leads to an unwarranted pessimism about Palestinian prospects. Of course, this is a time to take stock, and reformulate a vision and strategy to guide the Palestinian struggle. As the future is unknowable, such a call for strategic reset is not an occasion for optimism, it is rather a time for the renewal of struggle and for a deepening of solidarity on the part of those of us who seek justice for the Palestinian people. Yet this taking of stock must be as realistic as possible about the elements in the national, regional, and global context that pose challenges to the Palestine national movement.

Several adverse developments should be taken into account. First and foremost, Israel has successfully maintained, perhaps extended, its hard power dominance, including the acquisition of the latest weapons systems (e.g., Iron Dome), and become an arms supplier for over one hundred countries around the world ensuring a measure of political spillover. Second, Palestinian fragmentation and vulnerability have been accentuated by a series of policies: the split between Fatah and Hamas; the Oslo bisecting of the West Bank; the various divisions: between refugees and persons living under occupation, between West Bank and Gaza, between East Jerusalem and West Bank; between those dispossessed in 1948, 1967, and subsequently; between the Palestinian minority within 1967 "Green Line" and those living either under occupation or in exile. Third, the perpetuation of unconditional support by the US Government, especially Congress, which gives Israel little reason to feel bound by international law, UN authority, and international morality, and has resulted in impunity in relation to Israeli refusals to abide by international criminal law.

In effect, Israel has been able to rely on its capacity to contain Palestinian resistance by employing a mix of hard power capabilities backed up by a range of soft power instruments of control. Such an Israeli approach has included reliance on state terror to crush Palestinian resistance and a sophisticated *hasbara* campaign of disinformation, propaganda, and defamation of enemies to obscure the structures of violence and oppression that have been constructed to weaken, and if possible destroy, the Palestinian national movement.

This Israeli approach has been also extended to its relations with the Middle East in general, especially with respect to neighboring countries. Israel has used its hard power dominance and diplomatic skills to encourage fragmentation and to impart a disabling sense of utter vulnerability to any leadership in the region that dares challenge or threaten Israel. Iran has been the principal target of this Israeli projection of a tendency to punish disproportionately and violently those that stand in the way or exhibit hostility to the Israeli National Project, which has its regional dimensions. Syria is illustrative of the sort of fragmentation that weakens a neighboring country that has been hostile or in a conflictual relationship with Israel. A welcoming of the 2013 Egyptian coup that displaced the democratically elected government with an oppressive military leadership is a further disclosure of Israel's conception of its security interests.

Taking these various elements into account, as understood from a realist perspective that deems hard power as the main agent of history, Israel has achieved a strong sense of security, with little incentive to make concessions relating to Palestinian goals, grievances, and rights.

It is the inadequacy of such realism to comprehend the recent historic record of the failures of hard power superiority to sustain national security that is ironically the foundation of a hopeful future for the Palestinian people. Hope rests on the empirical validation of recent commitments to struggle, even uphill, for what is right, although not with any assurance of victory, which would amount to an embrace of an unwarranted optimism about the future.

The Palestinian Shift to Legitimacy War: Acknowledgement and Affirmation

I believe a crucial shift in Palestinian understanding about how to progress toward their goals has been taking place during recent years, and is being implemented in a variety of venues around the world. It is a shift in the direction toward greater reliance on a "Legitimacy War" being waged by the Palestinian people to secure their fundamental rights. The essence of this war, waged at many global sites of struggle, is to gain control over the discourse relating to international law, international morality, and human rights as it relates to the Israel–Palestine conflict. The discourse is also embedded in a revised tactical agenda that emphasizes two main elements: reliance on nonviolent initiatives of a militant character; and the social mobilization of a global solidarity movement committed to achieving self-determination for the Palestinian people. Such tactics range widely from hunger strikes in Israeli prisons, to efforts to break the blockade on Gaza, to pressures brought to bear from various constituencies on corporations and banks to break commercial connections with unlawful Israeli settlements or on popular cultural figures to forego invitations to perform in Israel.

In effect, the Legitimacy War being waged is seeking to rely on soft power instruments to exert mounting pressure on the Israeli government, creating incentives for Israel's elites to reassess their interests and policy alternatives. Such a reassessment would include an acknowledgement that past over-reliance on hard power superiority has produced new threats to Israel's longer term well-being, and even to security as understood in a wider sense as encompassing the ingredients of a peaceful and productive life that includes a sense of national self-esteem.

Legitimacy Wars shift the emphasis from *governments* and *governing elites* to *people* and *civil society* as the principal agents of historical change, and at the same time, in this instance, subordinate, but do not necessarily substitute, hard power forms of resistance to soft power tactics. There is no inherent commitment to nonviolence, but rather a matter of seeking an effective strategy in a particular context— what some describe as "smart power." This follows the guidance of Nelson Mandela and others that liberation movements should select their tactics on the basis of perceived *effectiveness* as contextually determined. Of course, even if it would seem that violence has a part to play, as was certainly the case for the Zionist movement of struggle against the British Mandate, there is still the legal/ethical questions associated with the selection of appropriate targets and the avoidance of operations directed at civilians, especially women and children. What appears to be the case in relation to Palestine is a definite move toward the adoption of a Legitimacy War conception of how to interpret the Palestinian national movement at the present time.

It seems important to understand, especially for non-Palestinians, that it is the Palestinians who should retain control over the discourse on their struggle and projection of vision and strategy. It is up to the rest of us, those who side with the Palestinians in the struggle to uphold their rights, that we not encroach on this political space, and appreciate that our role is secondary and derivative, to aid and abet, to accept a responsibility to act *in solidarity*. It is this kind of activist solidarity that will hasten a victorious trend in the Legitimacy War, with impacts in the behavioral domain wherein the materiality of change takes place. This important distinction between *resistance* and *solidarity* is a key to a successful embodiment of this shift by the Palestinian national movement.

In this regard, it should be remembered that ever since this encounter originated the Palestinian people have been victimized by outsiders acting to decide what was in their best national interest. If we go back to the Balfour Declaration, the British Mandate, the UN commission that devised the Partition Plan, and the various American formulations of how to resolve the conflict, the Palestinians are always treated as the objects never as the subjects of the peace process. Beyond this, this international paternalism, whether well meaning or not, has contributed to, rather than overcome, or even mitigated, the Palestinian tragedy.

Inter-governmental solidarity is also important for turning success in Legitimacy Wars into appropriate political outcomes. In this regard, it is regrettable that so few governments in the Middle East have exhibited solidarity in concrete and relevant forms in relation to this latest phase of the Palestinian national movement. It is not in the Palestinian interest to act as if the Oslo Framework or The Roadmap are any longer credible paths to a sustainable and just peace. The Palestinian people are entitled at this stage to more relevant forms of support in their struggle, and especially the people of Gaza should not be left to languish in an unfolding humanitarian catastrophe while diplomats dither in luxurious venues.

Finally, it is worth noting the historical trends since the end of World War II. By and large, the militarist side has not prevailed. This is true of the major anti-colonial wars. It is also true in the state–society struggles in Eastern Europe and the Soviet Union, and most of all in South Africa where a Legitimacy War strategy was largely responsible for the remarkable outcome that defied all expectations. America military dominance in Vietnam over the course of a decade did not produce victory, but a humiliating political defeat. True in the First Gulf War of 1991, the military superiority of coalition forces overwhelmed Saddam Hussein, and produced a political surrender, but that was a conflict in which the defensive response was wrongly rooted in contesting these vastly superior Western and regional forces on a desert battlefield where popular and unconventional forms of resistance were irrelevant. It is when the people become centrally engaged in a struggle that the political potency of soft power instruments is exhibited. Even when success is achieved in a legitimacy war it does not ensure victory in the political struggle as such cases as Tibet, Chechnya, Kashmir, among many others, including many of the struggles of native peoples, illustrate. What the turn toward Legitimacy Wars does achieve is a significant neutralization of hard power advantages in a political struggle involving such fundamental rights as that of self-determination. In this sense, it is most relevant to a reinterpretation of the vision and strategy of the Palestinian national movement.

This relevance is increasingly acknowledged by Israel itself, which has shifted its concerns from Palestinian armed resistance to what it calls "the Delegitimation Project" or "lawfare," terms that are given a negative spin as efforts to destroy Israel by relying on law and such challenges to Israeli legitimacy as mounted by the BDS Campaign. In effect, Israeli *hasbara* contend that Israel is being victimized by an *illegitimate* Legitimacy War, an argument American political leaders seem to accept, revealing their geopolitically conditioned support for international law and morality.

There are likely to be many developments in coming years as to the viability and effectiveness of the Palestinian engagement in a Legitimacy War against Israel. At present, it appears to be a unifying vision capable of restoring collective unity to the Palestinian national movement, and by so doing, bringing hope for a brighter Palestinian future.

Conclusion

A line taken from Mahmoud Darwish's poem, "Mahmoud Darwish Bids Edward Said Farewell," (translated by Mona Anis) expresses the central sentiment being affirmed by this approach:

There is no tomorrow in yesterday, so let us advance.

PART II

PALESTINE'S LEGITIMACY WAR

5

Violence and Nonviolence in the Palestinian Human Rights Struggle

(co-authored with Victoria Mason)

Introduction

"If only there was a Palestinian Gandhi." In recent years this has been a common sentiment expressed by leading international figures such as United States President Barak Obama.[1] This is part of a wider liberal argument that failures to establish a sustainable peace between Israel and the Palestinians are primarily a consequence of Palestinian terrorism, and that if the Palestinians would embrace nonviolence, they would gain the support of the international community—including the USA—as well as find a resonant response within Israel itself. In reality, however, Palestinians have a long history of relying on nonviolence to resist oppression and occupation, with armed struggle coming at a relatively late stage.[2] Yet those resisting the Israeli occupation through nonviolence have often been brutally repressed: being denied permits/ freedom of movement, humiliated, interrogated, subjected to night raids, arrested, jailed, beaten, and shot.[3] Compounding the Israeli response to Palestinian nonviolence has been the refusal of the international community to take notice, particularly in comparison to the extensive favorable global media coverage of nonviolent activism in the so-called "Arab Spring" (and the ruthless response by states such as Egypt, Syria, Bahrain, and Libya).

This invisibility, combined with the wider lack of action to uphold Palestinian rights, threatens the viability of this politics of nonviolence. After all, the efficacy of nonviolence as a strategy of struggle lies in its ability to either morally persuade the opponent to moderate its behavior (either directly or through a third-party intermediary); or for the nonviolent tactics to render the opponent's behavior too costly socially, economically, or politically for them to persist.[4] As Arundhati Roy argues, nonviolence is "a piece of theatre" and requires a responsive audience in order to be effective.[5] The lack of engagement with Palestinian nonviolence strips it of its transformative capability to alter the landscape of the Israeli–Palestinian conflict, particularly in terms of the impact of violence on both sides. In this chapter, we explore Palestinian use of both violence and nonviolence in their struggle. We then assess the potential of nonviolent action to end the occupation and achieve Palestinian rights in accordance with international law. Such an outcome would comprise a momentous step in resolving the wider Israeli–Palestinian conflict in a manner that enables a just peace for both parties.

Nonviolent Resistance

The perception that violence is the most effective means of action for resistance groups persists within mainstream international relations.[6] However, as demonstrated by Erica Chenoweth and Maria Stephan, nonviolent resistance is actually considerably more effective than its violent counterpart.[7] Their "Nonviolent and Violent Conflict Outcomes" (NAVCO) dataset examining 323 movements between the years of 1900 and 2006 found that nonviolent campaigns were successful 53 percent of the time, compared with just 26 percent for those that used violence.[8] It is therefore imperative to challenge dominant assumptions within international relations concerning the strategic value of nonviolent tactics.[9] Notwithstanding the ongoing definitional debates, nonviolence can broadly be characterized as a "method used to wage conflict through social, psychological, economic, and political means without the threat or use of violence" with the aim of mobilizing "publics to oppose or support different policies, to delegitimize adversaries, and to remove or restrict adversaries' sources of power."[10]

Within nonviolence there are two main approaches, summarized broadly as "principled nonviolence/pacifism" and "strategic/pragmatic" nonviolence. The former is where individuals or a group reject all forms of conflict and violence out of moral or religiously based belief.[11] Strategic, or pragmatic, nonviolence, on the other hand, sees struggle as necessary to end injustice and views nonviolence as the most effective tactic (morally and strategically) to this end.[12] It is crucial to differentiate between the two strands of nonviolence, as the conflation of the two traditions has led to criticisms that nonviolence as a movement constitutes neutrality at best, or at worst an out-of-touch, idealist, and even neo-colonial framework that advocates complicity and submission to injustice.[13] In reality, as the leading theorist on nonviolence, Gene Sharp, points out, "Non-violent action is a technique by which people who reject passivity and submission, and who see struggle as essential, can wage their conflict without violence."[14]

A wide range of nonviolent acts are possible, including "acts of omission, acts of commission, or a combination of both."[15] In Sharp's typology, there are three main categories of action: acts of protest or persuasion (such as marches and protests), noncooperation (such as boycotts and strikes), and intervention (such as civil disobedience, sit-ins, hunger-strikes and building parallel/alternative social institutions). Debates occur, of course, particularly between proponents of strategic and principled schools of thought, over whether certain acts can be considered nonviolent.[16] In such debates Wendy Pearlman reminds us that the wider context is crucial. For example, "for movements that espouse armed struggle, a shift toward stone throwing represents a decrease in the violent character of protest." If, on the other hand, a liberation struggle had been based previously on strikes and demonstrations, an embrace of stone-throwing would be a definite tactical move in the direction of armed struggle.[17] Broadly summarizing, Chenoweth and Stephan posit that nonviolent movements are those where there is a "primacy of nonviolent resistance methods and the nature of the participation in that form of resistance."[18]

The reality of conflict means that violent and nonviolent campaigns often occur contemporaneously by different groups, particularly if nonviolent action does not engender the sought-after response.[19] Indeed, as Sharp points out, if the conditions for the success of nonviolence are not found, some conflicts can only be resolved by armed struggle.[20] The literature on popular struggles against oppression similarly shows that patterns of resistance generally take the shape of a bell-curve, where "a small portion is collaborative, most of it nonviolent, some of it violent and some of it extremely violent."[21] Illustrative of this, recent struggles such as against apartheid South Africa, and as part of the civil rights movement in the USA, utilized both violent and nonviolent tactics, with each having varying levels of efficacy under different conditions. Likewise, Zionists utilized both violent and nonviolent means in their struggle for the establishment of the State of Israel,[22] and among Palestinians there has been support for both armed struggle and nonviolence, with levels shifting according to the perceived effectiveness of tactics at various times.[23]

The challenge then is to identify the circumstances under which nonviolence can be successful, and how best to bring about those conditions. Johan Galtung's work on how nonviolence acts to change the behavior of target state/regime/groups is seminal here. He first proposes "moral jujitsu," whereby nonviolent efforts aim to persuade and/or convert the thinking of the opponent—either directly or through influencing a third-party intermediary.[24] If the target regime/state/ actor is not converted, Galtung argues that strategies of nonviolence must move to "political jujitsu," or more coercive nonviolent tactics.[25] In this approach, the costs of maintaining the oppression need to become so prohibitive diplomatically, economically, socially, or psychologically that the target state/regime/group has no choice but to change their behavior.

Chenoweth and Stephan argue that such tactics are successful strategically as they generally: a) encourage broader participation within resistance amongst the aggrieved community; and b) confer greater legitimacy on a resistance group/movement (both domestically and internationally), therefore creating greater pressures on the state/ regime/group being targeted.[26] Both of these factors, however, are dependent on context. In terms of the first point, nonviolent movements are in theory able to recruit higher numbers of participants due to their tactics posing fewer risks, raising less moral quandaries, and generally allowing for physical participation amongst diverse demographics.[27] However, not all situations are conducive to this broad participation. For example, in the case study examined here, the spatial matrix of control established by Israel, especially since the Second Intifada— through the "Separation Wall," checkpoints, roadblocks, settler-only road networks, curfews, and closure policies—make mass physical mobilization by Palestinians (and Israelis and internationals who wish to act in nonviolent solidarity) very difficult.[28]

In terms of nonviolence conferring greater legitimacy on a movement, this requires moral and/or political jujitsu having a responsive audience either in terms of the targeted state/regime/group or third-party intermediaries.[29] One of the main ways in which this operates is through "backfire," if the state/regime/group chooses to respond to nonviolence with violence.[30] "Backfire" can have an impact both internally and externally. In terms of the former, orders for repressive measures against those utilizing nonviolence can convert the sympathies of individuals within the architecture of violence, leading to a "breakdown of obedience." This can see individuals/groups such as members of the military refusing to take part in the violence.[31] External backfire is also possible, eliciting the power of "shame" and resulting in international condemnation, diplomatic, financial, or other pressure (such as boycotts, divestments, and sanctions) against the targeted state/regime/group.[32] However, Sharon Erickson Nepstead and Lester Kurtz remind us that regimes/states can also quash nonviolence through less-obviously brutal, but similarly punitive, means, such as harsh economic oppression or covert funding aimed at "dividing and conquering" movements.[33]

Distilling the complexities of nonviolent action, the central elements required for nonviolence to succeed are: a) recognition of the use of nonviolent resistance by relevant audiences; and b) constructive responses to the nonviolence within the target state/regime/group and/or the international community. Without the existence of these two conditions, however, it is unlikely the nonviolent action will succeed, and in such situations, nonviolence may then give way to more violent means. On the basis of this discussion, we now briefly consider the evolution of Palestinian nonviolent resistance and its successes and frustrations, whether it is realistic to believe that nonviolence can bring about a just solution to the Palestinian situation, and what steps might be taken to this end.

Palestinian Resistance

While this chapter focuses on the use of nonviolence by the Palestinian people and the associated global movement to achieve Palestinian rights, it must be recognized that such an approach cannot prejudge other forms of resistance carried on within the limits of international law and in furtherance of the goals of global justice. The right to armed struggle, as outlined in the Geneva Convention Additional Protocols (Art. 1/4), with its specific reference to "armed conflicts in which peoples are fighting against colonial domination and alien occupation and against racist regimes in the exercise of their right of self-determination" has become an established norm of International Law.[34] Thus, as with all peoples, the rights of resistance belong to the Palestinian people and their representatives, with this reinforced by the near unanimous 2004 International Court of Justice (ICJ) Advisory Opinion on the legality of Israel's Separation Wall, which determined that Israel's right to security cannot be invoked to override the right of Palestinians to self-determination.[35] Furthermore, it is the right of the Palestinian people alone to decide how their right to self-determination can be most effectively exercised, within of course the constraints of International Humanitarian Law (IHL) and International Human Rights Law (IHRL).[36] As expressed by Ibrahim Shikaki, a youth organizer in Ramallah:

> there are attempts to impose the idea that non-violence is the only form of resistance "allowed," thus falsely implying that all other forms of resistance are ... immoral or illegal ... where ... the correct resistance method will demonstrate our worthiness to be given our rights and independence. Portraying our rights to freedom and self-determination as contingent upon our chosen method of resistance is at best inaccurate, and at worst rather racist. Implying that our rights have not been fulfilled because we have not demonstrated our worthiness of them relieves Israel of the need to uphold international law and grant us our basic rights, and also excuses Western hegemonies for awarding Israel full impunity to carry on with its violations and crimes.[37]

When Palestinians have used violence in their resistance struggle, they have received high levels of international attention and strong censure. This is entirely warranted where such attacks have violated international law, such as attacks on civilians. The historical focus on Palestinian violence, however—particularly without due attention to Israeli violence—fails to adequately recognize the origins of the conflict in the denial and abuse of Palestinian rights. As Secretary General of the UN Ban Ki-moon admitted in relation to the escalation of violence from October 2015, Palestinian anger:

> is bred from nearly five decades of Israeli occupation. It is the result of fear, humiliation, frustration and mistrust. It has been fed by the wounds of decades of bloody conflict, which will take a long time to heal. Palestinian youth in particular are tired of broken promises and they see no light at the end of the tunnel.[38]

The unswerving focus on Palestinian violence also fails to recognize that there has always been debate and division among the Palestinian people, and the various political factions, as to the most appropriate strategies and tactics for resistance, with support for both violence and nonviolence at various times.[39] Looking first to the use of violence, similarly to other resistance groups, a significant segment of Palestinian society (waxing and waning over time) have favored armed struggle, with violence playing a key role in the mythology surrounding Palestinian resistance.[40] Indeed, as a result of this, the *shahid* or "martyr" has become a seminal figure in Palestinian society.[41] At various times there has also been considerable support among Palestinians for actions that constitute terror attacks—such as suicide bombings—with the justification offered that such acts are one of the few tools available to the weak to offset the advantages of the strong.[42] This view has also at times led to suicide bombers being praised as heroic "martyrs,"[43] a position that has garnered significant attention and condemnation by the international community.

The equally significant history of Palestinian nonviolent resistance, however, is virtually unknown. In part this relative invisibility may reflect the reality that violence has far greater media appeal than nonviolence. For, as Mazin Qumsiyeh outlines, armed resistance by the Palestinian people to foreign intervention came at a relatively late stage:

> after 40 years of Zionist colonization. For the first few decades (1880s–1920s), all resistance was popular and unarmed. Later, all uprisings started as popular resistance, but some were marked by

armed resistance in response to the brutality of the occupiers and colonizers. As such, [Palestinian] armed resistance was limited, considering the injustice.[44]

Another major factor complicating the recognition of nonviolence by Palestinians has been that the term "nonviolence" (*la 'unf*) does not translate positively into Arabic—implying passivity and weakness. As a result, nonviolence as a concept is generally avoided in Palestinian commentary.[45] Instead, the spectrum of actions generally understood by the West to encompass "nonviolence" are described by Palestinians as "civil resistance," "political defiance," or "popular resistance" (*Muqawama sha'biya*) with the latter being the most widely used.[46] Yet many in the West interpret any form of political behavior that includes the word "resistance" as implying violence and have thus often misconstrued the Palestinian meaning of "popular resistance."[47]

Throughout its history, Palestinian nonviolence has evolved and adapted. While mostly comprising strategic nonviolence as a pragmatic adjustment to the asymmetry of the conflict with Israel, nonviolence has also been undertaken for principled and moral reasons.[48] As Palestinian political leader and scholar Hanan Ashrawi argues,

> Non-violence, as far as I'm concerned, has always been the most effective means ... because ... you have the moral high ground, in which you expose and you defy power and militarism and you expose the limits of power and the immorality of the [opponent] ... by being more moral than they are.[49]

Examples of nonviolent action by Palestinians can be traced back to Ottoman times, but became particularly relevant during the British Mandate, which saw resistance to British colonial control and support of Zionist aspirations in historic Palestine, as closely linked to Palestinian demands for political independence. A high-profile manifestation of nonviolence was evident in the 1936–1939 Arab Revolt, which was characterized by political entreaties, diplomatic petitions, protests, strikes, and other forms of civil disobedience.[50] These actions were met by a British colonial response that was "brutal, calculating and divisive." Thousands of Palestinians "were arrested for nothing more than voicing opposition or establishing political parties that challenged colonial rule. Those who resisted violently were hunted down and killed. Hangings were common."[51]

After the creation of the State of Israel in 1948, which gave rise to the *nakba* (catastrophe) in the form of the dispossession of 750,000–1,000,000 Palestinians,[52] the remnant of the Palestinian community in historic Palestine concentrated on survival under difficult conditions, either subject to Israeli military rule within the Green Line or living in a subjugated manner in areas administered by Jordan and Egypt.[53] Those Palestinians displaced to neighboring countries believed they would be imminently repatriated to their homeland in line with the guidelines set forth in UN Resolution 194. With the passage of time it became clear, however, that diplomatic initiatives were not going to result in the Palestinian Right of Return, and nearly seven decades later these Palestinians remain as refugees or in exile.[54]

Gradually the hopes of a "soft" resolution of the conflict vanished, leading the Palestinian people to perceive that their rights would depend on armed struggle, rather than the international community upholding international law. With this recognition, alongside nonviolent resistance, during the 1950s Palestinian *fedayeen* (guerrilla fighters) commenced armed struggle, launching raids into Israel from neighboring states.[55] Recourse to armed struggle by the resistance movement then intensified following the 1967 defeat of the coalition of neighboring Arab states that resulted in Israel's occupation of the West Bank, East Jerusalem, and Gaza.

In the years after 1967, Israeli military control over the Occupied Palestinian Territories (OPT) of the West Bank, East Jerusalem, and Gaza was reinforced and extended by the establishment of Israeli civilian settlements. Such transfers of civilian populations are illegal under Article 49(6) of the Fourth Geneva Convention. Overall, Israeli rule in the OPT was authoritarian and repressive: until 1993 Palestinians required permits for most aspects of everyday life; the promotion of self-determination was deemed criminal; the Palestinian economy was de-institutionalized and de-developed; dependence on the Israeli economy was entrenched, as was the exploitation of Palestinian labor.[56] Palestinian civil society organizations responded by undertaking both nonviolent and violent resistance. The nonviolent resistance included strikes, civil disobedience, non-cooperation with military officials, demonstrations and boycotts on providing labor to Israel, and the violent resistance included guerrilla attacks on Israel and the killings of suspected Palestinian "collaborators."[57] During this time, Palestinians also established a wide array of groups and associations aimed at both providing social services and setting the foundations for a quasi-state architecture in preparation for a future Palestinian state.[58] The determination of the Palestinian people to achieve political independence only increased as Israel attempted to suppress resistance through means such as curfews, harassment, mass arrests, and imprisonment (also incorporating "administrative detention" without charge or trial), house demolitions, and deportations.[59]

In 1973, Israel's victory in the Yom Kippur War marked the demise of efforts by neighboring Arab states to achieve Palestinian self-determination (amongst other more self-interested objectives) by militarily challenging Israel. With neither diplomatic attempts nor *fedayeen* attacks redressing Palestinian grievances, Palestinian armed struggle became more radical in the 1970s. This radicalization included Palestinian groups such as "Black September" undertaking acts such as the 1972 murder of Israeli athletes at the Munich Olympics.[60] Such actions greatly damaged the Palestinian cause, lending credibility to the Israeli insistence that Palestinian resistance was nothing more than a species of terrorism.[61] While such actions were indeed deplorable, there was no concomitant censure of Israel for its violations of international law through its increasingly oppressive occupation, unlawful settlement expansions, acts of ethnic cleansing in East Jerusalem, and refusal to implement the Right of Return for Palestinian refugees.[62]

A major turning point in the Palestinian struggle occurred as a result of the 1987 Intifada (uprising), where a traffic collision that killed four Palestinians brought discontent to the fore. Massive demonstrations broke out across the OPT and escalated into a sustained uprising involving people across all sections of Palestinian life. Palestinians took to the streets in huge numbers undertaking nonviolent actions such as: demonstrating; building barricades and road-blocks; burning tires; staging sit-ins; participating in strikes and other examples of civil disobedience; the development of household economies to increase self-reliance; wearing clothes in the Palestinian national colors; and raising the outlawed Palestinian flag.[63] Given the high rates of imprisonment and administrative detention of Palestinian men, major roles in the Intifada were played by women and youths, and it was, for the most part, unarmed, with Israel Defense Forces (IDF) documents classing 97 percent of the Intifada activities as nonviolent.[64]

A major form of protest—which came to symbolize the grass-roots nature of the uprising—was throwing stones at the Israeli security forces, which resulted in the Intifada being labeled the "Stone Revolution."[65] The Israeli government argued that the stone-throwing constituted violence, and it was regarded in this way by and large by the Israeli public.[66] Scholars such as Edward Kauffman have contended that the throwing of stones constituted the use of "limited" violence, and was ultimately counter-productive to the aims of Palestinian nonviolent resistance as it "distorted" the perception of the overall movement, and therefore lessened its ability to convert sympathies to the Palestinian struggle for rights.[67] Alternate arguments, however, are that given the asymmetry in the conflict, and that as the stone-throwing targeted highly weaponized Israeli military personnel and vehicles, it represented "but a symbolic gesture. It is a symbol of the vast discrepancy in power between the Palestinian people and Israel's war machine."[68]

The Stone Revolution was also notable in that it was an uprising that emerged from the grassroots, rather than from the formal Palestinian leadership. Indeed, the Intifada largely took the PLO by surprise, and they had to play "catch-up" to benefit from the gains of the popular movement.[69] Due in part to this swell of action of the Intifada, and in particular its impact symbolically, in 1988 the PLO and the Palestinian National Council (PNC) agreed to accept Israel as a legitimate state within the 1967 borders and to establish peace on this basis. This move resulted in the then US Secretary of State George Shultz un-banning direct US contact with the PLO. While Shultz's response was welcomed by the Palestinians, it was not seen as commensurate with the extent of the compromises offered by the PLO and PNC here. For the Palestinian declaration represented an enormous concession to the Israeli state, with the 1967 borders constituting less than half of what the UN General Assembly had allocated for the Palestinian state in 1947's UN Resolution 181.

As the uprising in the OPT continued, it was met with what the Israeli scholar Avi Shlaim has described as the "extreme" use "of force on a massive scale."[70] This included beatings (including the infamous order by the then Defence Minister Yitzhak Rabin to break the arms and legs of protesters), arrests, shootings, house demolitions, uprooting of trees, deportations, curfews, extended imprisonments, and detentions without trial, and the closure of Palestinian institutions such as schools.[71] During the first two years of the Intifada, around 500 Palestinians were killed, 7,000 were injured, and 50,000 were arrested.[72] This disproportionate use of violence arguably reflects a core Israeli strategy in relation to its conflicts both with Palestinians and the Arab states more widely—known as the "iron wall."

As Shlaim outlines, the iron wall stratagem emerged in the 1920s with Ze'ev Jabotinsky, who is widely considered to be the "father" of the Israeli political Right. The central tenets of the iron wall are that,

the Zionist project could only be implemented unilaterally and by military force. The crux ... was to enable the Zionist movement to deal with its local opponents from a position of unassailable strength ... Despair was expected to promote pragmatism on the other side and thus ... [opponents] learnt the hard way that Israel could not be defeated on the battlefield.[73]

Shlaim argues that the iron wall was adopted (in practice, if not in formal policy) by Israel from its early days.[74] Alongside the IDF actions on the ground detailed above, evidence that the iron wall was applied during the First Intifada is reflected in the rhetoric by Israeli leaders at the time. For example, the Israeli Prime Minister Yitzhak Shamir declared that "not one Arab would survive," if Palestinians started to use live weapons; and the Defence Minister Rabin "exhorted his troops to use 'might, force, beatings.'"[75]

In a classic illustration of "backfire," however, the use of the iron wall strategy by Israel damaged the state's international reputation. As Andrew Rigby outlines, the world's media presented images of "stone-throwing youths clashing with Israeli soldiers armed with tear-gas grenades, rubber-bullets and other weapons."[76] The shame effect of backfire led to a questioning of the dominant narrative that the Jewish state was the "David" fighting for survival against the Arab "Goliath" (including Palestinians) bent on their destruction.[77] This resulted in a shift in how the conflict was viewed throughout the world. One significant indicator of this shift was the UN Security

Council passing a resolution (without the USA exercising their veto) in December 1987, condemning Israel's use of disproportionate force.[78]

Many everyday Israelis were also shocked by their governments' repression, and this was a major factor in the subsequent election of a Labor government on a pro-peace platform. The Intifada also breathed new life into the Israeli peace movement, and resulted in increased solidarity activities between Israeli and Palestinian groups.[79] Shifts within Israel were also reflected by a growing number of '*refuseniks*'— Israelis who refused to serve in the IDF in the Occupied Territories on moral grounds—a key example of the effects of internal backfire and conversion of the opponent.[80]

These crucial shifts within Israel and internationally were central in creating the push for the 1992 Madrid Peace Conference.[81] Thus, despite the deep structural flaws in the Madrid process and subsequent peace initiatives, the Intifada serves as an example of the successful deployment of nonviolence in terms of creating moral shifts in the political climate and building pressure on target states/regimes/ groups both directly and by way of third-party intermediaries.

To begin with, the peace process initiated in Oslo was greeted with enthusiasm by most Palestinians and Israelis.[82] There were of course, peace "spoilers" on both sides—with Hamas's commencement of suicide bombings in 1993, and acts by extremist Israelis such as the massacre by Baruch Goldstein and the assassination of Prime Minister Yitzhak Rabin.[83] However, the initial optimism about the Oslo process soon diluted amongst Palestinians. A major factor in this was that the neo-realist power-politics approach of the peace process meant that it has sought to settle the Israeli–Palestinian conflict "based on the local balance of power" with prospective solutions "adapted more to the perception of the stronger party and less to that of the weaker party."[84] This, in combination with the USA playing the dual roles of chief mediator and closest ally of Israel, soon resulted in the peace process serving to consolidate and reflect the asymmetry of the two parties, with the core concerns of the Israeli state being given precedence over the concerns and rights of the Palestinians.[85] As this asymmetry became increasingly apparent in the years following 1993—particularly with the dramatic increase in settlement construction in the OPT—this period increasingly become known by Palestinians as the "Oslo Phase of the Occupation."[86]

Growing dissent amongst Palestinians toward the peace process resulted in a range of responses, both nonviolent and violent. The most visible of these responses, however, was Hamas's suicide bombings.[87] Deep frustration at the dramatic increase in settlements and overall expansion of the occupation during the peace process also contributed significantly to the eruption of the "Al-Aqsa Intifada."[88] This uprising was initially nonviolent.[89] The spur for the uprising was the then prime ministerial contender Ariel Sharon's visit to the Haram al-Sharif in September 2000, which Palestinians viewed as provocative. In the demonstrations that broke out on the next day, six Palestinians were killed and some 220 wounded (with 70 Israeli police also injured). For the first month of the uprising, Palestinians largely "refrained from using firearms," however "the Israeli army fired approximately 1.3 million bullets" in the OPT over the same period.[90]

At this point confrontations escalated into deadly uses of force by both sides—with a range of Palestinian groups launching terror attacks on Israeli civilians (including an average of 20 suicide bombing attacks a year) and Israel using helicopter gunships, tanks, missiles, targeted assassinations, and collective punishment.[91] Two images became symbolic of the vicious upswing in violence: the first being that of Muhammad al-Durrah, a 12-year-old Palestinian boy shot and killed by Israeli troops as his father tried to shield him; and the second, the lynching of IDF reservists by a Palestinian mob in Ramallah.[92] By conservative estimates, by the end of 2005, some 3,240 Palestinians and 950 Israelis (including soldiers) had been killed in the violence.[93] It also resulted in the "Israeli army recapturing the West Bank in an iron-fisted crackdown ... with colossal economic losses, territorial fragmentation and incalculable social suffering."[94]

However, alongside this violence, many Palestinians remained committed to nonviolent resistance. As documented by Maia Hallward and Julie Norman, Palestinian nonviolence included acts of protest, demonstrations, civil disobedience, boycotts of Israeli goods (particularly those produced in the settlements), providing legal clinics, and acts of solidarity and *sumud* (steadfastness).[95] These nonviolent efforts, however, received little recognition, and despite the much greater reliance on violence by Israel during this time, it was the Palestinians who bore the brunt of international condemnation.[96]

Hence the use of nonviolence during this time failed to achieve significant gains for the Palestinians.

Missed Opportunities: Ignoring Nonviolence

One consequence of the asymmetry of the violence of the Al-Aqsa Intifada was a clear Palestinian move back toward nonviolent tactics. Although this move was dictated primarily by reasons of stratagem, the shift was also influenced by questions of principle. For example, the use of suicide bombings as a tactic had been controversial both within Palestinian political factions, and the wider population, resulting in Hamas banning its use against civilians in 2006.[97] Such a development had significant potential to alter the landscape of the Israeli–Palestinian conflict, particularly with respect to its impact on civilians. Yet there was no constructive response. Despite the Israeli state and the international community continually insisting that Palestinian terror is a principal obstacle to peace, Palestinian shifts away from violence have not been acknowledged, much less reciprocated, and important opportunities to create a more peace-oriented dynamic have been overlooked. At the same time, moreover, Israel has consistently moved in the opposite direction, employing military might and unilateralism to consolidate their control of Palestinian territory and create "facts on the ground" that have all but destroyed Palestinian prospects for a viable and independent state.[98]

Despite the reality created by the occupation's facts on the ground, however, many Palestinians recognized that the use of violence during the Al-Aqsa Intifada was ultimately counter-productive. The asymmetry of the uprising meant that Israel dominated in violent encounters, yet the horror of suicide bombings led to international condemnation being largely directed at the Palestinians. Thus, the aftermath of the Intifada saw a greater reliance again on nonviolent tactics, with the Palestinian national movement again relying on protests, marches, demonstrations, civil disobedience, and hunger strikes.

Nonviolence has been particularly central to the campaign opposing the "Separation Wall" that Israel has been building since 2002, mostly on occupied Palestinian territory. The Israeli government disputes this name and calls it the "Security Barrier," arguing that it is constructed for security reasons, to protect Israelis from Palestinian armed attacks. However, 85 percent of the path of the Wall is built on Palestinian land, in some cases located as much as 22km inside the West Bank, incorporating that land into Israel. As a result, Israel is appropriating at least 10.1 percent of the West Bank, and in the process situating 85 percent of the illegal Israeli settlements on the Israeli side of the wall.[99] In 2004, the International Court of Justice (ICJ) concluded by a 14:1 vote,

> The construction of the wall ... and its associated régime, are contrary to international law ... [The ICJ] is not convinced that the specific course Israel has chosen for the wall was necessary to attain its security objectives ... the route chosen for the wall gives expression *in loco* to the illegal measures taken by Israel.[100]

Construction of the Wall has continued despite this near unanimous Advisory Opinion, its subsequent endorsement by the UN General Assembly, and the reality that it represents a continuing violation of the Israeli primary obligation under the Geneva Convention to protect the well-being of an occupied population.[101]

Nonviolence has also been practiced by Palestinians to oppose ongoing land and other resource confiscations, the expansion of settlements, house demolitions, and violence by settlers and Israeli security forces. Palestinians utilizing such nonviolent tactics, especially in public spaces, however, have been brutally repressed by Israeli forces, and sometimes by the Palestinian Authority's forces acting in cooperation with Israel in upholding "security" in West Bank urban centers.[102] Repression by the Israeli state has included activists being denied permits, being interrogated, subjected to night raids, arrested, jailed, and beaten.[103] One such example is that of activist Hamza Bornat, who in 2011 was sentenced to 18 months in prison and a 5,000 Israeli shekel (NIS) fine for filming footage on behalf of the West Bank village of Bil'in "Popular Committee Against the Wall and Settlements" (despite the fact that the Israeli High Court of Justice has ordered the Wall be less intrusively located in the case of Bil'in).[104] As a result of such actions, the Middle East Director at Human Rights Watch, Sarah Leah Whitson, has argued that: "the Israeli authorities are effectively banning peaceful expression of political speech by convicting supporters of non-violent resistance."[105]

In other examples of the violent suppression of nonviolent resistance, the weekly nonviolent demonstrations against the Wall are generally dispersed by the IDF "using tear-gas, rubber-coated steel bullets and chemical substances which cause nausea."[106] B'Tselem, a leading Israeli human rights group, has documented how between 2004 and 2007 alone, some 1,000 demonstrators needed medical treatment as a result of injuries from "bullets, beatings, or tear gas inhalation."[107] Such disproportionate use of force has often resulted in Palestinian youths throwing stones at the IDF. As discussed above, Israel contends that stone-throwing makes wider demonstrations "violent," however Palestinians argue that the "primary significance" of stone-throwing is that it is "a gesture of absolute defiance" in the face of unrelenting military force.[108]

In November 2014, the Israeli cabinet approved a law allowing jail sentences of up to 20 years for Palestinians throwing stones.[109] The resultant measures have included the jailing of a 14-year-old girl, Malik al-Khatib for two months (plus a 6,000NIS fine) and 15-year-old Khaled al-Sheikh for four months (with a 2,000NIS fine) for alleged stone-throwing—with both being convicted by military courts.[110] The Israeli government has also responded to more symbolic nonviolent actions, particularly those commemorating the Palestinian *nakba*, through so-called "lawfare." In March 2011, the Knesset passed the "*nakba* law," which enables the Israeli Finance Minister to reduce state funding or support to institutions that commemorate the *nakba* as a day of mourning.[111]

Possibly one of the most noteworthy examples of nonviolence in the face of adversity, however, has been Palestinians who have undertaken hunger strikes in response to being arrested and imprisoned under administrative detention by Israel. In their use of administrative detention, Israel as a matter of course holds Palestinians in prolonged detention without bringing them before courts to face charges and without revealing evidence or even allegations against them.[112] Detainees can be held for periods of up to six months, with the ability to extend this indefinitely.[113] While Israel as an occupying power under international law has the right to use administrative detention in situations of exceptional security threats, human rights organizations have demonstrated that its actual practice cannot be convincingly justified. According to B'Tselem:

given that administrative detention severely infringes the detainee's right to liberty and due process, the use of this power is subject to restrictions and stringent conditions. An examination of Israel's use of this power indicates, and at times decisively proves, that Israel violates these restrictions and conditions ... In many cases, the Israeli authorities use administrative detention as a rapid and efficient alternative to a criminal proceeding, especially when they do not have admissible evidence sufficient to convict the individual, or when they do not want to expose the evidence in their possession ... Israel has therefore made a charade out of the entire system of procedural safeguards in both domestic and international law regarding the right to liberty and due process.[114]

In recent years, a number of such Palestinians—notably Khader Adnan, Hana Shalabi, and Samer Issawi—have engaged in long hunger strikes to resist their detention. While Israel agreed to release several strikers reported by medical authorities to be close to death, they have also sometimes attached punitive conditions upon release, for instance, separating Hana Shalabi from her family in the West Bank by deporting her for three years to Gaza.[115] In July 2015, the Knesset moreover passed a law authorizing the force-feeding of hunger strikers, despite vehement opposition to this violation of rights by the Israel Medical Association, international medical authorities, and human rights NGOs.[116] Consistent with the wider pattern discussed in this paper has been the failure of the international community to give any substantial attention to the strikers. This is particularly remarkable given the keen interest shown to the 1981 Irish Republican Army (IRA) hunger strikes. The IRA strikes, and the international response to them, are regarded as at least partially responsible for changes in British policy at the time, particularly in terms of shifting its central effort from one of counter-insurgency to that of reconciliation, leading to the 1998 Good Friday Agreement.

Conclusion: No Peace Without Justice

What these examples show is that despite the perseverance of those engaged in the Palestinian nonviolent movement, non-responsiveness (and indeed measures designed to undermine nonviolent initiatives) threaten the viability of the entire movement. For all resistance movements will assess the efficacy of their strategies. To this end, some Palestinians feel that a posture of unreciprocated nonviolence constitutes surrender to subjugation, and disguised collaboration with Israel.[117] As Ashrawi points out, if nonviolence does not bring about concrete results for Palestinians:

> you cannot say keep using the same means if nobody reacts positively to you or listens to you ... the occupation is by definition violent, very violent, because you have to use violence to oppress a whole people. We are a captive nation. And so when you're facing it with non-violence, of course, if you produce results, if you expose it the way we did before [during the First Intifada], then that's fine. Then people see results. But if you don't, then people start picking up the same attitude as their oppressor, the same means, and this is where you begin to lose, unfortunately.[118]

This sidelining of nonviolence then risks widespread armed struggle by the Palestinians—with potentially devastating ramifications for Palestinians, Israelis, the Middle East region, and the wider globe. It is thus necessary to assess the potential for nonviolence to succeed in attaining Palestinian rights under international law.

Looking first to potential shifts by the Israeli government in relation to Palestinian rights, the current coalition is widely regarded as the most right-wing in the country's history, with leading Israeli commentators arguing that extremist trends in Israeli politics are no longer on the "fringes" but "in the mainstream."[119] Such trends have included inflammatory statements by some of the country's highest ranking government officials, including: Prime Minister Benjamin Netanyahu's 2015 vow to prevent the creation of a Palestinian state; the then Foreign Minister Avigdor Lieberman's call for "disloyal" Palestinians in Israel to be beheaded; the then Deputy Speaker of the Knesset Moshe Feiglin's call for Palestinians in Gaza to be put in concentration camps; and the current Justice Minister Ayelet Shaked's (then Minister of the Knesset) controversial 2014 social media post labeling all Palestinians as "snakes" and "enemy combatants" and arguing that "their blood shall be on their heads."[120] Consequently, it is unlikely that any significant shift in policy in relation to Palestinian rights will occur in the short term within the current Israeli government as a result of Palestinian nonviolent resistance.

Turning to the likelihood of Palestinian nonviolence and Israeli repression resulting in backfire and conversion within Israeli society, observers such as Neve Gordon and Gideon Levy contend that the nature of the Israeli occupation and its associated closure regime have resulted in many Israelis today having very little experience of, or interactions with Palestinians in the OPT unless they are in such confrontational situation as the IDF and the settlers.[121] They argue that as a result, everyday Israelis have become largely desensitized to the reality of the Palestinian situation except during periodic crises when their fears are activated and violence becomes the order of the day.[122] Hence the prospect of any significant civil movement within Israel pushing for change in policies toward Palestinian rights is unlikely at this juncture.

A litmus test of the potential for such movements was perhaps the July 2015 arson attack on a Palestinian home by extremist Israelis. The hate crime resulted in an 18-month-old Palestinian baby Ali Saad Dawabsha being burned alive and his father and mother later dying from their horrific injuries. Their four-year-old badly burned son is the only survivor of the attack. Within a matter of days, a stabbing attack on a gay pride parade by another Israeli extremist left the Israeli teenager Shira Banki dead.[123] While this was not the first such arson attack against a Palestinian home while its residents were inside,[124] this attack garnered significant outrage. Around 2,000 Israelis attended rallies in Tel Aviv and Jerusalem against the acts, with President Reuven Rivlin telling one rally that "flames of hatred have spread through our country, flames of violence, of hatred, of false and distorted beliefs."[125] However, perhaps demonstrating the limits of any shifts was the fact that protests by Palestinians against the killing of the baby resulted in two Palestinian youths being fatally shot by the IDF.[126] While suspects of the arson terror attack were arrested in late 2015, and are the first Jewish Israelis to be held under administrative detention, there has been significant criticism of the gag order surrounding the investigation.[127] The wave of violence which commenced in October 2015—which at the time of writing has claimed 116 Palestinian (including 79 alleged to have been carrying out/attempting attacks on Israelis) and 15 Israeli lives—and the almost singular focus on Palestinian acts of violence, to the exclusion of Israeli violence (particularly by Israeli settlers) suggests that little shifts have occurred in this respect.[128]

Moving then to assessing the potential of Palestinian nonviolence to secure the support of the international community for Palestinian rights, as demonstrated throughout this chapter, for the most part, this movement has been rendered invisible within the formal corridors of power. In recent years, however, there has been a growing recognition of the human rights violations perpetrated by Israel against the Palestinians within global civil society.[129] A number of nonviolent initiatives to this end have emerged. Some of the more high profile of these include: the Russell Tribunal on Palestine; the "Freedom Flotillas"; "accompaniment and defensive" action taken by Israelis and internationals in conjunction with Palestinians; and the global Boycott, Divestment and Sanctions movement (BDS).

The Russell Tribunal aims to mobilize action in situations where impunity for violations of international law occurs "due to a lack of political will" by the international community. In 2009, the Russell Tribunal on Palestine was established as a means to push for concrete action in response to the 2004 International Court of Justice (ICJ) Advisory Opinion on the Separation Wall, and to end impunity for violations committed during the 2008–2009 war on Gaza.[130] While the Tribunal does not possess the legal jurisdiction to implement its recommendations, the hearings on Palestine have provided important expert testimony and evidence of human rights violations, and a basis for popular nonviolent mobilization.[131]

In terms of actions on the ground, organizations such as Christian Peacemakers, the Ecumenical Accompaniment Program in Palestine and Israel (EAPPI), and the International Solidarity Movement (ISM) have also played a central role in the Palestinian rights movement.[132] For example, established in 2001 by a collective of Palestinian, Israeli and international activists, the ISM posits that it aims to resist:

> the long-entrenched and systematic oppression and dispossession of the Palestinian population, using non-violent, direct-action methods and principles ... ISM aims to support and strengthen the Palestinian popular resistance by being immediately alongside Palestinians in olive groves, on school runs, at demonstrations, within villages being attacked, by houses being demolished or where Palestinians

are subject to consistent harassment or attacks from soldiers and settlers as well as numerous other situations.[133]

While such groups have provided witness to human rights violations, and mitigated violations to some extent by acting as "human shields," such groups themselves have experienced significant violence. A number of ISM activists have been injured by both the IDF and settlers—including the controversial killings of Rachel Corrie and Tom Hurndall by the IDF while they were acting as human shields in 2003.[134]

A further effort has been a succession of Flotillas endeavoring to break the blockade of Gaza.[135] These Flotillas have aimed to deliver humanitarian aid and construction materials to the Gaza Strip, and to draw global attention to the blockade. They have, however, been prevented from reaching Gaza by the Israeli military, including through the illegal boarding of vessels in international waters and the use of excessive force by the IDF. This includes the now notorious 2010 Mavi Marmara incident, which resulted in the killing of nine flotilla activists (and the wounding of many more) and injuries to IDF members.[136]

Given Israel's response to such initiatives, many within global civil society argue that at present the most viable nonviolent option in the struggle for Palestinian rights is the Boycott, Divestment, and Sanctions (BDS) movement.[137] Respected international figures, such as Archbishop Desmond Tutu, advance that:

> those who continue to do business with Israel, who contribute to a sense of "normalcy" in Israeli society, are doing the people of Israel and Palestine a disservice. They are contributing to the perpetuation of a profoundly unjust status quo. Those who contribute to Israel's temporary isolation are saying that Israelis and Palestinians are equally entitled to dignity and peace ... It is becoming more and more clear that politicians and diplomats are failing to come up with answers, and that responsibility for brokering a sustainable solution to the crisis in the Holy Land rests with civil society and the people of Israel and Palestine themselves.[138]

Proponents of BDS argue that it is a powerful, nonviolent tool, moored in principles of human rights (and similar to strategies used successfully against Apartheid South Africa), to pressure Israel to adhere to international law by making it too costly economically and in terms of Israel's status and reputation within the international community.[139] The movement has been vehemently denounced by Israel, which argues that it is anti-Semitic.[140] However, supporters of BDS contend that this charge is an attempt to use spurious accusations of anti-Semitism as a trope of silencing to inhibit discussion, support, and participation in BDS.[141] Proponents argue that Israel is seeking to discredit BDS precisely because it represents such a potentially effective nonviolent strategy.[142]

According to the movement literature, BDS aims to address the maintenance, defense, and consolidation of right violations through:

i.   Boycotts of "products and companies (Israeli and international) that profit from the violation of Palestinian rights" and "Israeli cultural and academic institutions" that "directly contribute to maintaining, defending or whitewashing the oppression of Palestinians"

ii. Divestment from "corporations complicit in the violation of Palestinian rights"

iii. Sanctions against Israel until Palestinian rights are upheld "in full compliance with international law."[143]

Ashrawi argues that far from the demonization of BDS by the Israeli government, "the movement does not target Jews, individually or collectively, and rejects all forms of bigotry and discrimination, including anti-Semitism."[144] Examples of the institutions targeted by BDS include Israeli academic institutions with linkages to the Israeli military and/or which are complicit in the occupation (such as Bar Ilan University, which collaborates with a college in the illegal settlement of Ariel); businesses that are based in illegal settlements such as Soda Stream; corporations such as Caterpillar that provide specially designed equipment to bulldoze Palestinian houses; and businesses that donate money to the Israeli military (such as the Israeli-owned Max Brenner chocolate company).

Recent BDS successes include significant international divestments from companies regarded as complicit in the occupation—such as G4S, Caterpillar, Hewlett Packard, and Motorola, and in July 2014, twelve European Union states released statements warning their citizens not to become involved in businesses linked to settlements due to their illegality under international law.[145] Key religious bodies such as the United States United Church of Christ, the World Council of Churches, the Church of Scotland, and the Presbyterian Church (USA), and an increasing number of university bodies have moreover voted to divest or cease cooperation with Israeli and/or foreign entities that are complicit in the violation of Palestinian rights.[146] In this vein, there have also been increasing calls for imposing an arms embargo on Israel both as consumer and dealer, as well as a rising effort in the USA to question its annual military assistance program to Israel.[147]

While the BDS movement is experiencing significant success, 2014 and 2015 have seen increasing spirals of violence, and at present the Palestinian nonviolent movement faces increasingly insurmountable barriers. This puts the international community at a crossroads. As an editorial in *The Economist* back in 2011 argues in impressive language:

We've asked the Palestinians to lay down their arms. We've told them their lack of a state is their own fault; if only they would embrace non-violence, a reasonable and unprejudiced world would see the merit of their claims ... If crowds of tens of thousands of non-violent Palestinian protestors continue to march, and if Israel continues to shoot at them, what will we do? Will we make good on our rhetoric, and press Israel to give them their state? Or will it turn out that our paeans to non-violence were just cynical tactics in an amoral international power contest staged by militaristic Israeli and American right-wing groups whose elective affinities lead them to shape a common narrative of the alien Arab/Muslim threat? Will we even bother to acknowledge that the Palestinians are protesting non-violently? Or will we soldier on with the same empty decades-old rhetoric, now drained of any truth or meaning, because it protects established relationships of power? What will it take to ... recognize that the real Martin Luther King-style non-violent

Palestinian protestors have arrived, and that Israeli soldiers are shooting them with real bullets?[148]

The success of Palestinian nonviolence depends on whether it engenders a constructive response, which is something that today presents a significant challenge to governments, international institutions, and global civil society.

6

International Law, Apartheid, and Israeli Responses to BDS

Introductory Perspectives

By now there are overwhelming confirmations that a just and sustainable peace between Palestine and Israel will not be achieved by traditional diplomacy or through the efforts of the United Nations. Justice will be eventually achieved, but only through the agency of struggle waged by, with, and on behalf of the Palestinian people. This is the primary lesson of more than 60 years of Palestinian dispossession resulting in massive exile and huge refugee encampments. Furthermore, since 1967, an oppressive occupation has morphed into an apartheid regime of colonialist governance and a creeping form of de facto annexation facilitated by the establishment and expansion of unlawful Israeli settlements throughout the West Bank and East Jerusalem. The secondary lesson is that neither the United States nor the UN has been able or willing to counter Israeli criminal defiance of international law and the related impunity of their leaders. Perhaps most tellingly, the world watched as helpless spectators while Israel mercilessly attacked Gaza for three weeks at the end of 2008, and then again in 2012, and in 2014 for 51 days with the most devastating results. On each of these occasions, Israel deployed the full panoply of modern weaponry, much of it supplied by the United States, to wage this series of one-sided wars against a vulnerable population recalling some of the worst colonialist excesses.

With shades of irony, Israel used this battlefield experience as part of the sales pitch of its robust export arms industry, claiming field-tested weapons and tactics as a major selling point to those many governments facing an internal insurgent threat.

With this experience of decades of Palestinian suffering and frustration, the cruel charade of a recurrent "peace process" should no longer delude people around the world that an end to the Palestinian ordeal can be brought about by the leaders of these two embattled peoples, and their American intermediary whose consistent partisanship contradicts its self-serving claim to act as an honest broker. At the same time, there are encouraging signs on the political horizons that give hope and direction to the Palestinian struggle: despite its counter-revolutionary reversal, the "Arab Spring" reminds us that even the most oppressive and abusive forms of political rule are potentially vulnerable to massive popular uprisings by brave and determined nonviolent collective action. At present, the Palestinian outlook is not favorable, given several recent regional and global developments. The reversal of the Arab Spring restored autocratic governance throughout the Middle East, and had the effect of inducing governments in the region to erode further their solidarity with the Palestinians struggle. A further political setback for the Palestinians has been the resumption of normalized political relations between Turkey and Israel.

Despite these adverse developments, there has been a continuing build-up of civil society support for the Palestinian national movement. This support has been mainly visible in the form of an expanding and deepening global Palestinian Solidarity Movement (PSM). How this shift from inter-governmental diplomacy to civil society activism will play out in the future seems quite uncertain at present.

With this background in mind, we can assess this increasingly robust PSM that has as its central expression the BDS (Boycott, Divestment, and Sanctions) Campaign. This campaign, initiated by a coalition of more than 170 Palestinian NGOs, has been inspired by, but not copied from, the South African anti-apartheid campaign that was so effective in discrediting and isolating the racist regime in Pretoria, paving the way with minimal violence toward the establishment of a multi-racial constitutional democracy led by Nelson Mandela. The South African experience, while different in crucial respects, does underscore the degree to which the militarily weaker and politically oppressed side in a prolonged conflict can prevail if its cause is just, it persists in struggle, and it relies on appropriate tactics.

Launching the BDS Campaign represented a shift in the priorities of resistance for Palestinian society, featuring a reduced reliance on governmental initiatives (politics from above) and a new confidence in the historical agency of popular movements (politics from below), without rejecting some combination of the two in the final phases of a push toward peace and self-determination. BDS, although seeking a political climate more conducive to balanced diplomacy at the level of sovereign states, presently insists that only the mobilization and activism of civil society can uphold Palestinian rights. In this regard, BDS represents a major commitment to soft power approaches to conflict resolution, although not necessarily involving the unconditional renunciation of armed resistance. BDS is itself a nonviolent form of political activism that relies on the voluntary participation of people at all levels of society, regardless of their national or ethnic identities, and without geographical limitations. Its origins, leadership, and orientation are Palestinian, but its recruitment and range of actions are ecumenical and flexible with respect to the degrees of commitment that are understood to reflect the diverse outlooks of participating actors and their program. The campaign is as wide as the world, issuing a special welcome to its ranks to members of Israeli society. Indeed, Israeli participation is valued highly in the BDS movement. It has an enhanced symbolic and substantive status because the defection of Israelis, whether rightly or wrongly, tends to lend an added measure of authenticity to the justice and reasonableness of Palestinian claims, demands, and tactics.

Although the movement supporting BDS is global in scope and composed of peoples of many national, ethnic, and religious identities, it is important for non-Palestinian supporters to accept that its direction and political approach should always remain under the direction of its Palestinian organizers. It is important in this regard that those of us who are not Palestinian, yet lend support to BDS, reject Orientalist efforts to substitute our West-centric guidance for theirs. In this regard, non-Palestinians active in the PSM have a political responsibility to defer to the lead of Palestinian civil society who currently best represent Palestinian democratic aspirations.

Legality of BDS

The essential character of the international BDS campaign is an expression of citizens in a free society to demonstrate their moral concerns, and to appeal to others to join them. Seeking to promote the rights of the Palestinian people under international law is thus integral to the functioning of a democratic society. It is nonviolent and relies on persuasion to achieve its desired results. It is also educational, as it needs to convince people why BDS is appropriate. International law does not explicitly validate BDS by name, although clearly it stands as an expression of fundamental civil and political rights that are enumerated in the Universal Declaration of Human Rights and subsequent treaty instruments.

The imposition of sanctions by governments does raise some legal issues, although these are not normally viewed as serious impediments to the adoption of sanctions. It can be argued that sanctions violate the non-intervention norm in international law if imposed by government action as was the case during the last stages of the anti-apartheid campaign. If sanctions are decreed by the UN Security Council, as is presently the case with respect to Iran, it constitutes a controversial challenge to Article 2(7) of the Charter that prohibits UN intervention in matters essentially within the domestic jurisdiction of a state unless international peace and security are found to be seriously at stake.

A Tool Against Apartheid (Again)?

At the same time, the South African precedent is relevant in several respects, especially in giving its legitimating blessings to nonviolent forms of global initiatives against a racist regime by a member state that failed to abide by international law, ignoring a variety of UN initiatives including the disregard of the International Crime of the Suppression and Punishment of the Crime of Apartheid (1973). The BDS campaign argues that among the most serious Israeli forms of criminal unlawfulness is the multi-dimensional imposition of an apartheid regime that consists of the discriminatory separation of Palestinians into such subordinated categories as occupied, refugee, terrorist, and minority in a Jewish state. It is important to appreciate that international law treats "apartheid" as a universal crime, and not one that necessarily resembles the forms of drastic discrimination that prevailed in South Africa.

The generalizing of the crime of apartheid was given treaty form in the International Convention on the Suppression and Punishment of the Crime of Apartheid, which came into force in 1973 with adherences now numbering 107 states. The crime of apartheid is defined in the Convention as "inhuman acts for the purpose of establishing and maintaining domination by one racial group of persons over any other racial group and systematically oppressing them."[1] The Rome Statute of the International Criminal Court treats apartheid as one of seven forms of Crimes Against Humanity, describing its essence as consisting of an "institutionalized regime of systematic oppression and domination by one racial group."[2]

The most obviously apartheid structure has evolved in the West Bank where a dual system of administration accords full legal protection to Israeli settlers, while subjecting Palestinians to a non-accountable Israeli administrative regime of military occupation that was established in 1967, and has gradually matured into de facto annexation.[3] The apartheid character of this occupation regime is associated with several features of the Israeli–Palestinian relationship:

- preferential citizenship, visitation, family unification, and residence laws and practices that prevent Palestinians who reside in the West Bank or Gaza or elsewhere in the world from reclaiming their property lost in 1948, 1967 or at other times, or from acquiring Israeli citizenship or even residence rights, as contrasted to a Jewish right of return that entitles Jews anywhere in the world with no prior tie to Israel to visit, reside, obtain property, and become Israeli citizens;
- differential systems of authority in the West Bank favoring Jewish settlers (inhabiting settlements that were established in flagrant and continuing violation of Article 49(6) of the Fourth Geneva Convention) who enjoy full rights under Israeli law, as opposed to Palestinian residents living in the same geographic space and with full legal rights to be there, who are governed by military administration that is arbitrary and abusive;
- dual and discriminatory arrangements for movement in the West Bank and to and from Jerusalem, including an Israeli-only road network and a separation wall determined unlawful by the World Court in 2004; discriminatory policies on land ownership, tenure, and use; extensive burdening of Palestinian movement, including checkpoints involving long waits and frequent

humiliations for Palestinians while Israeli settlers and visitors have unrestricted mobility facilitated by different colored license plates on cars; also, there are onerous permit and identification requirements imposed only on Palestinians;

- Palestinians are subject to punitive house demolitions, expulsions, deportations, and restrictions on entry to and exit from all three parts of Occupied Palestine. Israel exercises full control over 60 percent of the West Bank area, and has recently been imposing a variety of conditions on Bedouin communities near Jerusalem and in the Negev with the thinly disguised objective of dispossessing them. In contrast, Israeli settlers live securely including those who have established settler outposts, which although illegal under Israeli law as well as international law, receive protection from Israeli military forces and are awarded subsidies from government ministries involved in housing.

In short, Israeli apartheid structures, policies, and practices are pervasive in their dual character, producing gross economic, social, and political inequality between Israelis and Palestinians. These structures have evolved over time and assume different forms in the West Bank and East Jerusalem, as well as in Israel itself. With some irony, blockaded Gaza is the only portion of Occupied Palestine that does not have to cope with everyday apartheid, although the oppressive and multiply dangerous quality of life in Gaza makes its "imprisoned" population possibly the most victimized of all Palestinian constituencies at the present time. It should be remembered in the BDS context that apartheid is universally treated as an international crime, and that by making support for BDS a civil wrong, Israel is seeking to discourage nonviolent opposition to crime by imposing harsh penalties.

There is also the related issue of the Palestinian minority within Israel. There is an increasing insistence by the Israeli government that it be recognized as "a Jewish state," not only by the leadership representing the Palestinian people in international negotiations and the international community, but even by its 1.7 million Palestinian Israeli citizens, which amounts to about 20 percent of Israel's total population. These Palestinian citizens of Israel are subject to a large variety of discriminatory laws and regulations, open discussion of their being transferred to a Palestinian entity without their consent, and greater scrutiny than Israelis with respect to mobility. This may or may not amount to "apartheid," but it illustrates and confirms the systematically racist nature of the treatment inflicted upon the Palestinians for more than six decades.

Contending that BDS is Anti-Semitic or "Racist"

Some critics of BDS insist that by focusing on Israel there is a selectivity of concerns that targets the "Jewish state" of Israel while neglecting comparable or worse infringements on international law and human rights elsewhere in the world, and that as a result BDS should be viewed as anti-Semitic or racist. The literature and rationale for BDS is based on the rights of Palestinian people and stands or falls on its own. The entire international community has been preoccupied with the Israel–Palestine conflict for some decades, and the whole foundation of Israel's existence rests on initiatives of the United Nations and external actors. The International Court of Justice in 2004 issued a near unanimous Advisory Opinion, expressing the clear conclusions that Israel had a solemn obligation to abide by international law in its relations with the Palestinian people.[4] Israel repudiated this authoritative judgment, and continued to flaunt international law by continuing with the construction of the wall, thereby disregarding the rights of the Palestinian people.

There is also the initial colonialist commitment of the Balfour Declaration in 1917 that looked with favor at the establishment of "a national home for the Jewish people" (not "state") in historic Palestine, "it being clearly understood that nothing should be done which may prejudice the civil and religious rights of existing non-Jewish communities."[5] In this manner, Britain conditioned the fulfillment of the Zionist project by reference to the protection of Palestinian rights, an obligation that was later transferred to the UN when Britain ended their role as mandatory power. It is the failure to uphold this obligation over such a long period that has both generated Palestinian resistance and struggle, and led over time to a widening circle of global civil society initiatives undertaken in solidarity with the Palestinian people of which BDS and the Freedom Flotillas are recent examples.

It is pure diversion on the part of supporters of Israel to charge anti-Semitism under these circumstances. Israel's flagrant violation of international law, its refusal to respect Palestinian rights, its strong linkage to the United States, and the unfulfilled UN role fully justify the attention given to the conflict. BDS is fully consistent with international law, and reflects the values of democratic engagement of peoples beyond borders in struggles for global justice.

Israeli Responses to BDS

It is worth noting that the more seriously framed Israeli objections to BDS are not based on appeals to international law, but are rather political and moral arguments contending that BDS, despite its claims to be promoting human rights and global justice, is actually part of an effort to delegitimize Israel's "right to exist." A further claim is that BDS supporters often call for the resolution of the conflict by way of a one-state solution, although the campaign itself focuses on the achievement of Palestinian rights without taking a position on the shape of the future Palestinian state, which is arguably premised on the replacement of the present Israeli state by a secular bi-national state.[6]

Israel has increasingly associated the BDS Campaign with what it refers to as the "Delegitimization" of Israel. The most analytical and comprehensive assessment along these lines has been prepared by the Israeli think-tank, The Reut Institute.[7] The basic contention is that the BDS Campaign, whether consciously or not, is seeking to question the legitimacy of Israel, as now constituted, and in their words "supersede the Zionist model with a state that is based on the 'one person, one vote' principle."[8] Given the BDS emphasis on Palestinian rights as the necessary precondition for a sustainable peace, the Reut position makes a reasonable case, although there is some ambiguity present. Shlomo Avineri, the prominent Israeli philosopher and political personality, has commended the distinction between challenging specific policies of Israel as illegitimate and questioning the Israeli state as such.[9] In effect, Israel will aggravate its problems of positive branding if it treats critics of its specific policies as equivalent to delegitimizers that question the viability of the Israeli state as it is now constituted. It seems difficult at this stage of the conflict, and given Israel's deliberate policies of expansionist settlement in the West Bank and East Jerusalem, to envisage any satisfactory resolution of the conflict except through the establishment of some form of bi-national secular state that is not organized along religious or ethnic exclusivist principles, although establishing homelands for both Jews and Palestinians.

The Reut Institute analysis also calls upon Israel to mount a counter-campaign that rebrands Israel positively in world public opinion, and reaffirms the Zionist essence of the Israeli state. It criticizes Israel's current foreign policy and security doctrine for its failure to respond appropriately to the "existential threat" posed by BDS, and more generally "the delegitimizers," reminding readers that powerful regimes have been undermined in the past, citing the South African experience during the apartheid period. The Reut call is for a worldwide counter-campaign that aims to isolate and discredit the delegitimizers, and restore the image of Israel by a global public relations (*hasbara*) mobilization, including activating Zionist communities throughout the world.[10] It also calls for reform in the Ministry of Foreign Affairs so that it can defend Israel against soft power tactics, and not reduce security to its traditional hard power dimensions. In this regard, the Reut approach recognizes the shift in Palestinian strategy, as exemplified by BDS, and complains that the Israeli Government has not reacted appropriately. I believe Tel Aviv has heeded this message, and is now itself making an all-out effort along the lines proposed by Reut, and is above all seeking to confuse this nonviolent struggle for Palestinian rights under international law by labeling BDS supporters as extremists and by insisting that systemic criticisms of Israel amount to a contemporary form of anti-Semitism.

In this sense, the battlefield associated with the Israel–Palestine conflict has been expanded in two dimensions: from a fundamentally territorial encounter between occupier and occupied to a worldwide struggle without boundaries; and from an emphasis on hard power oppression and hard power modes of resistance to a soft power competition based on controlling the heights of moral and legal authority as reinforced by public opinion and media sympathies.[11] It is not surprising that in this new phase of the struggle legal/moral issues such as the Goldstone Report, the flotilla incidents, and the BDS campaign have substantially displaced the dynamics of violent encounter.[12] In one sense, this itself is a victory of BDS, both by its recognition that Palestinian prospects depended on redefining the forms of engagement in the battle and by the Israeli admissions that they needed to change their own strategic orientation toward the conflict to avoid isolation and potential defeat. It could be also observed that such Israeli military initiatives as the Lebanon invasion of 2006 and Operation Cast Lead of 2008–2009 reached "frustrating outcomes" in the words of the Reut report,[13] and reflected an outdated and evidently dysfunctional militarist approach to Israel's true security and foreign policy interests.

Other purportedly moderate critics of BDS have emphasized such issues as scaring off mainstream peace advocates, undermining the Israeli peace movement that is generally opposed to boycott and divestment initiatives, and somehow feeding accusations of anti-Semitism through actions seen as highly critical of Israel.[14] Suffice to say after such prolonged failures at the inter-governmental level to secure fundamental Palestinian rights by relying on diplomatic approaches, it would seem entirely justifiable for those in solidarity with the Palestinian struggle and for Palestinian civil society activists to resort to such nonviolent coercive approaches to encourage compliance with international law. BDS represents an extraordinary campaign to address an extraordinary situation of prolonged oppressive occupation, colonization, apartheid, refugee and exile confinement, and denial of human rights, including the right of self-determination. As was the case with South Africa, apologists for Israel's policies seek to invoke such diversionary arguments to avoid the build-up of pressure for changes in governmental policy.

One recent Israeli response, reflecting the rightward drift of Israeli politics, is to pass an anti-boycott law titled "Bill for Prevention of Damage to the State of Israel Through Boycott 2011," on July 11, 2011 by a Knesset vote of 47:38. It makes supporters of BDS, including NGOs and even consumers in any form, subject to serious civil penalties of various kinds, and gives the sellers of boycotted goods a civil law remedy by showing damages. The scope of the law is very broad, penalizing any person or organization that advocates an "economic, cultural or academic boycott," and extending its reach explicitly to include settlement-only boycotts by saying that the penalties and rights of lawsuits apply if the boycott is directed towards products or services from "an area under its [Israel's] control."[15]

Under the law, individuals or organizations promoting a boycott, even if limited to settlement products, face lawsuits, denial of tax exemptions and other benefits from the state, and exclusion from bids for government contracts.[16] The removal of tax-exempt status, which can be decreed by the Israeli government, would make it difficult for some Israeli human rights groups to survive, and this may be a collateral goal of the legislation. The law explicitly protects a range of named settlement goods. It also prohibits the government from dealing with a foreign government or any company anywhere in the world that complies with any facet of the anti-Israel boycott. The backers of the anti-boycott law do not stress economic concerns as much as viewing this pushback against BDS as part of an effort by Israel to resist any further delegitimization, but I would think that this crude anti-boycott pushback measure will instead produce a surge of support for BDS initiatives around the world. Ironically, the unintended result of the anti-boycott law may be to lend an extra degree of legitimacy to the BDS campaign.

This Knesset action, legally controversial in Israel and among its international supporters, raises new issues about the branding of Israel as "the only democracy in the Middle East." This was never a credible claim but rather a triumph of Israeli *hasbara*, although much of Israel's new legislation including the anti-boycott bill exhibit increasing hostility to the freedoms associated with a genuine democracy.

Conclusion

The Palestinian BDS campaign owes its inspiration to the Anti-Apartheid Movement that adopted similar tactics from 1959 onwards that were seen as instrumental in reconstituting the political climate in such a manner so as to lead to an abandonment of racism, and the peaceful transformation of the South African constitutional structure in the direction of a multi-racial democracy. The South African outcome represents an extraordinary victory for soft power militancy, overcoming the cruel and comprehensively repressive apartheid regime. The BDS dimensions of the global solidarity movement was greatly strengthened by near universal support in the United Nations, and through the success of grass-roots anti-apartheid pressures in the United States and the United Kingdom in turning the two most important strategic allies of South Africa into supporters of international sanctions against the regime.

Even as the Palestinians are winning in the struggle for legitimacy in relation to their rights, and their demands for a just and sustainable peace, there are concerns about the political outcome of this latest phase of struggle. So far, Israel has been able to retain the support of the United States and most of Europe, and has been able to neutralize the United Nations to a large degree particularly though US vetoes in the Security Council and by its leverage within the UN bureaucracy. Furthermore, the Israeli leadership and public opinion show no signs of any willingness to consider options that acknowledge fundamental Palestinian rights, although this was also true in South Africa until an abrupt shift of opinion took place that had been entirely unexpected by informed outside observers. It should be realized that winning the Legitimacy War may not be enough. It has not been enough, for instance, to emancipate the people of Tibet or Chechnya.

At the same time, we cannot know the future. These nonviolent initiatives encompassed by BDS provide a legally and morally appropriate means to carry on the struggle for Palestinian rights. Such soft power tactics give Israel the opportunity to reconsider its approach to relations with the Palestinian people. The BDS mobilization, assuming that its momentum continues to build, creates incentives for Israel to consider more benign alternatives for its own future social, economic, and political development. In these respects, the BDS movement is a creative and constructive response to the challenges associated with the continuing denial of the most basic of Palestinian rights, and deserves the support of persons and governments supportive of human dignity and conscience throughout the world.

Such a conclusion is bolstered by the degree to which Israel has itself attuned its tactics to fighting against what it calls the Delegitimation Project of its opponents. In effect, Israel is recognizing that the main war zone is now subject to an encounter between soft power capabilities, and has started to appreciate that its hard power disposition and inclinations are no longer functional, although reliance on hard power tactics continues to dominate Israeli security thought and practice as the 2011 encounters at the borders with Lebanon and Syria exhibited.[17] The Palestinian refugees who were injured and killed by Israeli forces on Nakba Day and also in June were attempting to implement their rights as laid out by UN Resolutions, International Law and Human Rights legislation to return to their homes.

Always, the oppressed are waging an uphill battle against the structures and techniques of oppression. The Palestinians have been engaged in this struggle for many decades, but seem finally to have chosen an approach that takes advantage of their control of the moral and legal high ground. Israel foolishly reinforces this advantage by their consistent refusal to comply with international humanitarian law and human rights law, as well as their unwillingness to address Palestinian claims of right. History has normally vindicated perseverance in the struggle for basic rights, and the Palestinian movement for peace and justice is from one perspective the last major unfinished chapter in the anti-colonial narrative that was the dominant development supportive of human well-being in the last century. The BDS campaign is a hopeful way of writing the future history of Palestine in the legal and moral language of rights rather than in the bloody deeds of warfare. Such struggles, rooted so firmly in the arena of rights, deserve support from all of us.

7

Palestinian Lawfare and the Search for a Just Peace

The idea of using law as a policy instrument has existed as long as sovereign states engaged in relations with one another. The term "lawfare" has entered political discourse recently with both positive and negative inflections, and has been especially relied upon to discredit claims of legal right put forward by weaker actors involved in political struggle. In this way, lawfare is invoked to discredit claims based on international law advanced on behalf of the Palestinian people, almost as if it were an improper "weapon" in asymmetric warfare that if invoked is declared to disrupt a "peace process" based on diplomatic bargaining and not rights under international law.

"Lawfare" is treated by Israel as a bad word, denoting recourse to international law and the UN system for irresponsible purposes, including the delegitimation of Israeli policies and practices. This is unfortunate. Recourse to law and legal remedies in international life functions on behalf of the Palestinians as a preferred alternative to either "armed struggle" or a failed diplomacy. Lawfare understood as the reliance on international law and international institutions has increasingly functioned as a principal mode of resistance against a prolonged occupation and an Israeli pattern of defying its obligations under international law. Lawfare also identifies the contours of a peace process that can operate more effectively than the Oslo framework that since 1993 has excluded considerations of international law in the diplomacy of direct negotiations between the parties. In these respects, lawfare should be viewed as a positive word from the perspective of promoting the peaceful and just resolution of international disputes.

Lawfare in the context of controversy about the status of Israeli settlements emphasizes the strong international consensus supportive of the conclusion of illegality based, above all, on the prohibition of

Article 49(6) of the Fourth Geneva Convention and on the applicability of the Geneva Conventions and international humanitarian law to disputes about Israel's prolonged occupation of the West Bank, East Jerusalem, and Gaza. The prohibition forbids the transfer of the population of an occupying power to the territory of an occupied society. It has been explicitly affirmed as applicable to Israel's occupation of Palestine in the near unanimous ICJ Advisory Opinion of 2004 on Israel's Separation Wall as well as by reports and findings of inquiries carried on under the auspices of the UN Human Rights Council. Such a prohibition is further reinforced by the November 29, 2012 General Assembly resolution recognizing Palestine as a non-member state within the UN System and by the subsequent trend among European states confirming Palestinian statehood, reinforced most recently by the Vatican's formal recognition of Palestine.

Under present circumstances, both the International Court of Justice (ICJ) and the International Criminal Court (ICC) should be jurisdictionally available to pronounce upon aspects of Israel's occupation policy. There are limits to this availability with respect to the ICJ due to the presumed unwillingness of Israel to agree on the submission of a dispute with Palestine to this pre-eminent UN judicial body. A second limitation arises from the limits on the advisory function of the ICJ, as illustrated by the non-implementation reception of the recommendations in its 2004 Advisory Opinion, which confuses the interpretation of the word "advisory" with the idea of compliance being "voluntary." Recourse to the ICC is more promising but also is confronted by significant *political* limitations: Israeli non-cooperation; lack of enforcement capabilities; Israeli and US intense opposition and threatened retaliatory moves; and the possibility of a biased and selective application of international criminal law due to geopolitical pressures exerted on the ICC, leading it to conclude that only Hamas is guilty of violations.

Even adherence by Palestine to the Rome Treaty governing the operations of the ICC has brought charges by Israel that such an initiative is disruptive of the peace process and a negotiated solution of the conflict. It is to be expected that Israel would defy any judgment by the ICC adverse to its occupation policies and practices bearing on the status and character of the settlements. Further, based on past behavior,

Israel would retaliate by accelerating settlement expansion activities, possibly giving formal approval for additional construction and even legalizing the over 100 "outposts" currently illegal under Israeli law, although despite this, they are the beneficiaries of security protection and financial support. Israeli leaders that are potentially responsible for crimes against the Palestinian people enjoy a condition of de facto impunity, which further complicates any project to impose accountability by reliance on available legal mechanisms, including the ICC.

This prospect of Israeli non-compliance plus its threatened retaliatory moves raises fundamental questions as to why seek such legal remedies given the practical obstacles and generally such unfavorable circumstances. A responsible assessment should not blindly exhibit support for the undertaking of lawfare, if the consequences are likely to be negative. With eyes wide open, we need to ask "What is to be gained?"

The first line of response is that recourse to the ICC, and possibly even the ICJ, would be an expression by the Palestinian Authority of no confidence in further negotiations carried on within the Oslo framework. This diplomacy has been relied upon for almost 25 years. It has functioned to trap those representing the Palestinian people. It has weakened their prospects for a genuine peace and diminished Palestine's effective territorial presence. Further, a principal mode that this weakening has assumed over the years has been the continuous expansion of unlawful settlement activities without any effort by the intermediary to protect Palestinian rights or some expression of an Israeli willingness to accept the applicability of international humanitarian law (IHL) with respect to the settlements.

The second line of response is that a favorable outcome on the status of settlements would exert a significant impact on world public opinion within the UN, among governments especially in Europe, and in civil society, and that such impacts over time are likely to produce a diplomatic climate more conducive to generating a genuine peace process.

The third line of response is that there is much to be gained by establishing within an authoritative legal venue the *criminality of allegations* demonstrating that settlements have become integral to the apartheid character of the occupation regime that was established in

1967, and has intensified its systematic and discriminatory features during the course of the occupation.

Public opinion, as responsive to authoritative legal findings, contributes to the formation of international attitudes toward legitimacy and illegitimacy with respect to contested settlement policies in civil society and among governments. Past initiatives including the Goldstone Report and the Chantal Report[1] on settlements have strengthened pro-Palestinian legitimacy claims that combine having the support of law and morality. This support has resulted in some practical diplomatic gains, including an upgraded Palestinian status within the UN, the inter-governmental trend toward the recognition of Palestine as a state, and the strengthening of the BDS campaign internationally. The overall purpose of relying on international legal mechanisms in the absence of prospects for compliance is to alter the political climate in ways that make the realization of Palestinian rights, including the right of self-determination, more probable. The settlements issue has the potential to highlight the injustice and untenable nature of the present situation, and should be given emphasis to revive the international consensus in favor of "two states" and give greater weight to the global solidarity movement that aims to exert pressure on Israel to change its approach. In this regard, civil society tribunals can also play a constructive role in highlighting Israel's failure to fulfill its basic obligations under international law and as a Member of the United Nations. The four sessions on Palestine held under the auspices of the Russell Foundation in Brussels played a constructive role in reinforcing the relevance of international law, especially with regard to the apartheid character of the administration of the West Bank, recalling that apartheid is listed as a crime against humanity in Article 7(h) of the Rome Treaty. Such tribunals perform a lawfare function when international institutions and national governments are neutralized by political obstacles which preclude responsible action on behalf of vulnerable peoples whose rights are being systematically violated.

It is to be noted that within civil society, including within the United States, there is growing support for global solidarity activities supportive of Palestinian rights under international law—a trend especially visible among the college students and in mainstream church settings. In conclusion, lawfare as a major dimension of the current phase of the Palestinian national movement has a positive role to play, and from such a perspective, the criminal legality of Israel's settlement policies and practices can be considered "low hanging fruit," by wide agreement in serious violation of Israel's international obligations as an Occupying Power as this is understood within the Fourth Geneva Convention devoted to the obligations of a belligerent occupant.

8

Palestine Becomes a State

On November 29, 2012 the UN General Assembly voted 138:9 to upgrade the status of Palestine from being a "permanent observer entity" to that of "non-member statehood." The date had symbolic significance as it is the UN official "Day of Solidarity with the Palestinian People," observed in many places around the world, underscoring the plight of millions of Palestinians living under occupation, often as refugees, and many others scattered in an involuntary Palestinian diaspora throughout the world, a set of dismal conditions endured by some of the Palestinian people since the *nakba* of 1948 and for the rest (other than the 1.5 million living as a discriminated against minority within Israel) since the Six-Day War of 1967.

The initial reaction among Palestinians was to declare victory, and to celebrate this symbolic recognition as a political step closer to the goal of self-determination, expressed by way of the establishment of a sovereign Palestinian state within secured and acknowledged borders associated with the 1967 "Green Line," and including having its capital in Jerusalem, either in joint administration with Israel or in that part of the city known as East Jerusalem, and occupied by Israel since 1967.

It should be realized that this move by the Palestinian Liberation Organization and the Palestinian Authority in the General Assembly was a sequel to the stalled effort in 2011 to achieve full-fledged UN membership. This initiative, eloquently presented to the world community by Mahmoud Abbas in his speech on November 29, 2012 to the General Assembly, was blocked, as had been anticipated by the United States, which threatened to cast a veto if necessary to ensure that the membership (which implied statehood) bid did not go forward. The preferred mode of the United States was to bottle up the issue indefinitely in the tangled procedures of the UN bureaucracy, which it succeeded in doing, raising serious questions about the ability of a single powerful state to control the operations of the Organization on matters such as membership, which should not depend on the presence of a geopolitical consensus among the permanent members of the Security Council. Such a threatened use of the veto power, while technically consistent with the UN constitutional framework, is highly irresponsible, and should signal other countries to circumscribe the use of the veto along with other reforms that would make the UN Security Council more responsive to the needs and values of the organized world community in the early twenty-first century.

Few on either side of the controversy over Palestinian statehood paused to evaluate its real effects on the long struggle to realize Palestinian rights. On the Palestinian side, many assumed that any measure that was so intensely opposed by Israel, and its junior partner, the United States, must be of benefit to the Palestinians. Hamas reinforced this understanding by abandoning its original opposition to the statehood bid to one of political support, part of a renewed politics of reconciliation as between Fatah and Hamas. Although a Hamas spokesperson clarified this show of support by saying that it should not be understood as waiving its objections to the establishment of a Jewish state in historic Palestine, but nevertheless it was a momentous step toward achieving a compromise on Palestinian goals that corresponded to the global consensus on a two-state solution as articulated originally in Security Council Resolution 242 adopted unanimously in 1967, and numerous subsequent reaffirmations, including by Israeli and American political leaders. On his part, President Abbas made very clear the realistic scope of Palestinian ambitions when he said in his speech to the General Assembly, "we do not seek to delegitimize an existing state—that is Israel: but rather assert the state that must be realized—that is, Palestine."[1]

More questionably, in contrast with the language of the statehood resolution (UN General Assembly Resolution A/67/L.28, November 29, 2012),[2] Abbas in a recent interview seemed to imply a waiver of Palestinian rights of return when he said that he made no claim of a right to return to his birthplace in Safed, a town in pre-1967 Israel, although he would look forward in the future to the opportunity for a visit. The UN resolution, in contrast to such an imprudent weakening of refugee rights, refers to the resolution of the refugee problem "in conformity with resolution 194(III)," which unequivocally confirms the Palestinian right of return. Such a right is declaratory of international law on the matter. It is important that the text of the statehood resolution did not foster the impression that the establishment of Palestine as a state was *only* about "land for peace," with an abandonment of non-territorial demands.

Israel and the United States argue without any qualifications that Palestinian statehood can only be achieved by direct negotiations between the parties. Any effort to reach such an outcome by a shortcut or symbolically is, in the words of Susan Rice, US Ambassador to the UN, "unfortunate and counterproductive," as well as creating "further obstacles in the path of peace."[3] President Obama and his then Secretary of State, Hillary Clinton, all uttered this mantra of opposition whenever the Palestinians sought to enhance their status as a political actor. This is a diplomatic posture that seems cruel and unreasonable for at least two principal reasons: first, there is scant prospect for negotiations, which have been suspended since they collapsed in September 2010 when the Israeli Prime Minister, Benjamin Netanyahu refused to extend the moratorium on settlement expansion, and since then steadfastly refused to suspend settlement building even while negotiations are in progress while at the same time cynically calling for negotiations "without preconditions"; and second, the reality of an occupation that has lasted since 1967, and shows no credible signs of ending in the foreseeable future, makes it humane and reasonable to take some compensatory steps that might at least offer the protection of the daily rights of the Palestinian people as well as uphold their collective dignity while subject to an occupation that looks more and more like annexation. International humanitarian law, including the Fourth Geneva Convention and the Geneva Protocols of 1977, are deficient to the extent that they do not make special provisions on behalf of a civilian population entrapped in an ordeal of "prolonged occupation."

The Israeli response to the statehood bid is as disproportionate as is their uses of force contra Palestinians in the name of security. Israel has announced a series of accelerated and controversial settlement moves that annoyed even Washington, and antagonized Israel's supporters in Western Europe. So far announced, justified as a reaction to the General Assembly vote, was the approval of 3,000 housing units in the long deferred E1 settlement that has the effect of isolating Palestinian neighborhoods in East Jerusalem from the West Bank. Additionally,

Israel has also declared that it was moving toward final approval for an additional 1,500 units in the Ramo Shlomo settlement located in north Jerusalem. It is my view that Israel used the statehood vote as a pretext for retaliation so as to proceed with the accelerated expansion of the settlement phenomenon, which was part of its game plan in any event. On another level, this form of response is a further expression of Israeli rejection of UN (and international law) authority as it directly flaunts the clear language of the resolution, which calls for the "complete cessation of all Israeli settlement activities in the Occupied Palestinian Territories, including East Jerusalem."[4]

The deeper issues as to the value of this statehood resolution remain uncertain and contested. It does not dramatically alter the role of Palestine within the UN, which since 1998 has extended special privileges not available to other actors with an observer status, including the right to participate in the general debate at the start of all General Assembly annual sessions, as well as the right to co-sponsor resolutions. The further rights that membership in the UN would confer include the right to vote and to initiate resolutions and other activities. Depending on how statehood is used in the UN System, it could give the Palestinians options to join other actors that determine access by statehood criteria rather than on the basis of UN membership. This includes the International Criminal Court, and such specialized agencies as the International Labor Organization, World Health Organization, and the IMF and World Bank. It also gives Palestine the opportunity to adhere to human rights treaties, and build a stronger normative foundation for their claims to become a truly sovereign state that is a constructive member of international society.

Beyond this, prolonged occupation of a political entity that constitutes a state in the eyes of the United Nations would seem to open Israel to contentions that it is seeking in violation of a series of fundamental rules of international law to the contrary, including Charter Article 2(4), reaffirmed in the statehood resolution, and SC Resolution 242, to the effect that it is inadmissible to acquire territory by force. Especially in light of such extensive and sustained unlawful settlement activity, as well as the separation barrier and ethnic cleansing in Jerusalem, it would seem appropriate for the General Assembly to follow up with a resolution requesting an Advisory Opinion from the International

Court of Justice as to the legality of continued Israeli occupation of the West Bank, East Jerusalem, and Gaza in light of Palestinian statehood.

Palestinian statehood issues have an uncertain and somewhat indefinite relevance to the wider protection of Palestinian rights and the strengthening of international law and the United Nations. Complex issues of representation, as well as the confusing situation of Palestinian nationality, given the multiple residential circumstances in which Palestinians are forced to live, are explored with unsurpassed clarity and depth. The clarification of these concerns is relevant to the Palestinian struggle for self-determination, and has become a pragmatic point of departure for understanding several critical international law issues that have emerged in recent years.

Beyond the direct implications of the attainment of some degree of Palestinian statehood within the UN system remain the fundamental questions bearing on the prospects for achieving a just and sustainable outcome in relation to the underlying conflict with Israel. The statehood resolution reaffirmed the two-state consensus and The Quartet's endorsement of "The Roadmap," which to many seemed increasingly a cruel and deceptive desert mirage that had little prospect of being realized in a manner that would lead to a viable and independent sovereign Palestinian state. What self-determination might mean in light of this background where the two-state solution, as backed by an international consensus, seems to be nearing the end of its sunset phase and the one-state secular democracy alternative is generally put to one side in deference to the strong Zionist commitment to a Jewish state by the overwhelming majority of Israelis is an open question. In the present setting, it has become also necessary to contemplate a one-state imposed Israeli solution that seeks to deny forever the right of self-determination to the Palestinian people.

9

Seeking Vindication at the International Criminal Court

Ever since this latest Israeli major military operation against Gaza started back in 2014 there have been frequent suggestions that Israel is guilty of war crimes, and that Palestine should do its best to activate the International Criminal Court (ICC) on its behalf. The evidence overwhelmingly supports basic Palestinian allegations—Israel is guilty either of aggression in violation of the UN Charter or is in flagrant violation of its obligations as the Occupying Power under the Geneva Convention to protect the civilian population of an Occupied People; Israel seems guilty of using excessive and disproportionate force against a defenseless society in the Gaza Strip; and Israel, among an array of other offenses, seems guilty of committing Crimes Against Humanity in the form of imposing an apartheid regime in the West Bank and through the transfer of population to an occupied territory as it has proceeded with its massive settlement project.

Considering this background of apparent Israeli criminality, it would seem a no brainer for the Palestinian Authority to seek the help of the ICC in waging its struggle to win over world public opinion to their struggle. After all, the Palestinians are without military or diplomatic capabilities to oppose Israel, and on law and global solidarity must rest their hopes for eventually realizing their rights, particularly the right of self-determination. Such reasoning is reinforced by the May 8, 2016 letter sent by 17 respected human rights NGOs to President Mahmoud Abbas urging Palestine to become a member of the ICC, and act to end Israel's impunity. This was not a grandstanding gesture dreamed up on the irresponsible political margins of society. Among the signatories were such human rights stalwarts as Human Rights Watch, Amnesty International, Al-Haq, and the International Commission of Jurists— entities known for their prudence.

Adding further credence to the idea that the ICC option should be explored was the intense opposition by Israel and the United States, ominously threatening the PA with dire consequences if it tried to join the ICC, much less to seek justice through its activation. The then American ambassador to the UN, Samantha Power, herself long ago prominent as a human rights advocate, revealed Washington's nervous hand when she confessed that the ICC "is something that really poses a profound threat to Israel."[1] I am not sure that Power would like to live with the idea that because Israel is so vulnerable to mounting a legal challenge that its impunity must be upheld whatever the embarrassment of doing so. France and Germany have been more circumspect, saying absurdly that recourse to the ICC by Palestine should be avoided because it would disrupt "the final status negotiations," as if there have ever been any of value, a chimera if there ever was one.

In a better world, the Palestinian Authority (PA) would not hesitate to invoke the authority of the ICC, but in the world as it is, the decision is not so simple. To begin with, is the question of access, which is limited to states. Back in 2009, the PA tried to adhere to the Rome Statute, which is the treaty governing the ICC, and was rebuffed by the prosecutor who turned the issue over to the Security Council, claiming a lack of authority to determine whether the PA represented a "state." Subsequently, on November 29, 2012 the UN General Assembly overwhelmingly recognized Palestine as "a non-Member Observer State." Luis Moreno-Ocampo, who had acted in 2009 for the ICC, and now the former prosecutor, asserted that in his opinion, in view of the General Assembly action, Palestine would qualify as a state with the rights of ICC membership. Normally, ICC jurisdiction is limited to crimes committed *after* the state becomes a member, but there is a provision that enables a declaration to be made accepting jurisdiction for crimes committed at any date in its territory so long as it is after the ICC was established, which was 2002.

Is this enough? Israel has never become a party to the Rome Statute setting up the ICC, and would certainly refuse to cooperate with a prosecutor who sought to investigate war crimes charges with the possible intention of prosecution. In this regard, recourse to ICC might appear to be futile as even if arrest warrants were to be issued by the court, as was done in relation to Qaddafi and his son in 2011, there would be no prospect that the accused Israeli political and military figures would be handed over, and without the presence of such defendants in the court at The Hague, a criminal trial cannot go forward. This illustrates a basic problem with the enforcement of international criminal law. It has been effective only against the losers in wars or those whose crimes are in countries of the South. This has been true since the first major effort was made after World War II at Nuremberg and Tokyo, holding surviving German and Japanese leaders responsible for their crimes while exempting the winners, despite their responsibility for the systematic bombing of civilian populations by way of strategic bombing and the dropping of the atomic bombs on Hiroshima and Nagasaki.

Unfortunately, up to this time, the ICC has not been able to get rid of this legacy of "victors' justice," which has harmed its credibility and reputation. All ICC cases so far have involved accused from sub-Saharan African countries. The refusal of the ICC to investigate allegations of war crimes in relation to the Iraq War of 2003 is a dramatic confirmation that leading states, especially the United States, possess a geopolitical veto over what the ICC can do. The ICC failure to investigate the crimes of Bush and Blair, as well as their entourage, vividly shows the operations of double standards. Perhaps, the climate of opinion has evolved to the point where there would be an impulse to investigate the charges against Israel even if procedural obstacles preventing the case could not be carried to completion. Any serious attempt would add legitimacy to the Palestinian struggle, and might have a positive spillover effect on the global solidarity movement and the intensifying BDS campaign.

Yet there are other roadblocks. First of all, the PA would definitely have to be prepared to deal with the wrath of Israel, undoubtedly supported by the United States and more blandly by several European countries. The push back could go in either of two directions: Israel formally annexing most or all of the West Bank, or more likely, withholding the transfer of funds needed by the PA to support its operations. The US Congress would be certain to follow the lead of Tel Aviv, even if the Obama presidency might be more inclined to limit its opposition to a diplomatic slap on the wrist, as it did recently in reacting to the formation of the interim unity government that is attempting to reconcile Fatah and Hamas. Confirmation of this greater intensity of support for Israel in Congress as compared to the White

House was evident in late 2016 when the United States broke with its past practice, and abstained from Security Council Resolution 2334 (December 23, 2016) censuring Israel for obstructing prospects for peace by continuing with the expansion of unlawful settlements. Congress was highly critical of this move, regarding it as anti-Israeli and inconsistent with "the special relationship" between the two countries. President-elect Donald Trump also was highly critical of this move by the Obama presidency in its last weeks in office, suggesting policies toward Israel-Palestine more in line with the approach taken by the US Congress.

A second potential obstacle concerns the jurisdictional authority of the ICC, which extends to all war crimes committed on the territory of a treaty member, which means that leaders of Hamas could well be investigated and indicted for their reliance on indiscriminate rockets aimed in the direction of Israeli civilian targets.

There is even speculation that the politics of the ICC is such that crimes alleged against Hamas might be given priority.

If we assume that these obstacles have been considered, and Palestine still wants to go ahead with efforts to activate the investigation of war crimes in Gaza, and also in the rest of occupied Palestine, what then? And assume further, that the ICC reacts responsibly, and gives most of its attention to the allegations directed against Israel, the political actor that controls most aspects of the relationship. There are several major crimes against humanity enumerated in Articles 5-9 of the Rome Statute for which there exists abundant evidence as to make indictment and conviction all but inevitable if Palestine uses its privilege to activate an investigation and somehow is able to produce the defendants to face trial: reliance on excessive force, imposing an apartheid regime, collective punishment, and population transfers in relation to settlements.

The underlying criminality of the recent aggression associated with Protective Edge (Israel's name for the 2014 Gaza attack) cannot be investigated at this point by the ICC, and this seriously limits its authority. It was only in 2010 that an amendment was adopted by the required 2:3 majority of the 122 treaty members on an agreed definition of aggression, but it will not be operative until 2017. In this respect, there is a big hole in the coverage of war crimes currently within the authority of the ICC.

Despite all these problems, recourse to the ICC remains a valuable trump card in the PA deck, and playing it might begin to change the balance of forces bearing on the conflict that has for decades now denied the Palestinian people their basic rights under international law. If this should happen, it would also be a great challenge and opportunity for the ICC finally to override the geopolitical veto that has so far kept criminal accountability within the tight circle of "victors' justice" and hence only accorded the peoples of the world a very power-laden experience of justice.

PART III

ZIONISM AND ANTI-SEMITISM IN
THE INTERNATIONAL ARENA

10

Zionism and the United Nations

Zionism as Racism? Zionism and the State of Israel

More than 40 years ago the UN General Assembly adopted controversial Resolution 3379 by a vote of 72:35 (with 32 abstentions), determining "that Zionism is a form of racism and racial discrimination." This resolution was bitterly opposed by Israel and its friends in 1975. According to Zionists and others, this resolution was an unacceptable assault on the dignity of the Jewish people, a blatant expression of anti-Semitism, exhibiting hurtful insensitivity to the long dark shadow cast by horrific memories of the Holocaust.

The Israeli ambassador at the United Nations, Chaim Herzog, was unsparing in his denunciation: "For us, the Jewish people, this resolution based on hatred, falsehood and arrogance, is devoid of any moral or legal value." The American Ambassador, with a deserved reputation as an outspoken diplomat, Daniel Patrick Moynihan, was hardly less severe. In the debate preceding the vote, Moynihan used exaggerated language of denunciation: "The UN is about to make anti-Semitism international law. ... The [US] does not acknowledge, it will not abide by, it will never acquiesce in this infamous act ... a great evil has been loosed upon the world."[1]

Such harsh language was an effective tactical maneuver by Israel and the United States to mislead as to the purpose of the anti-Zionist resolution by waving the red flag of anti-Semitism. With a few notable exceptions, the governmental supporters of the initiative at the UN were never motivated by hatred of Jews, although the resolution was an unwise way to exhibit anger toward Israel because it was so susceptible to being discredited as unacceptable due to its alleged anti-Semitic overtones. The primary backers of the resolution were seeking to call attention to the fact that Israel as a state was proceeding in a racist manner by its treatment of the indigenous Palestinian population. In fact, the focus on Zionism rather than Israel reflected a continuing commitment by the main representatives of the Palestinian people and their allies to accept, however reluctantly, the reality of Israel as a state, while rejecting certain of its policies and practices that were being attributed to the Zionist ideology that did, and continue to, shape Israel's governing process.

The context of the resolution is also important. It came after a decade of international frustration concerning the refusal of Israel to withdraw from the Palestinian (and Syrian) territory occupied in the 1967 War in the manner prescribed in the unanimously passed iconic UN Security Resolution 242. By 1975, it seemed that Israel had no serious intention of ever withdrawing fully or soon. True, there were interpretative ambiguities surrounding the exact conditions of withdrawal, yet Israel's expansion of the metropolitan area of Jerusalem together with the establishment of settlements in occupied Palestine were generally perceived in UN circles as confirming this suspicion that Israeli ambitions far exceeded the scope of what had been agreed upon in 1967 at the Security Council. Subsequent developments have only hardened the perception of the belief that Israel will defy international law and UN authority whenever it suits their purposes.

Inappropriately and ineffectively, the anti-Zionist resolution was seeking to mobilize the international community in 1975 around the idea that Palestinian suffering and humiliation resulted from illegitimate Israeli behavior that would not be overcome by statecraft or UN diplomacy, both of which had been tried and failed. Over time this interpretation of the situation has given rise to a growing skepticism about whether any inter-governmental effort, including that undertaken by the Palestinians themselves, would lead to the exercise of the Palestinian right of self-determination, as long as the balance of forces is so strongly in Israel's favor. Against this background, it is not surprising that the Palestinian struggle increasingly relies upon civil society militancy currently epitomized by the BDS Campaign to correct this imbalance.

Asserting its geopolitical muscle over the years, Israel finally managed to induce the General Assembly to repudiate the anti-Zionist resolution in 1991 by Resolution 46/86. The single sentence text of the resolution simply revokes the earlier resolution that condemned Israel without offering any explanation for the change of position at the UN.

Israel secured this vote by making it a condition for its participation at the Madrid Peace Conference that same year, insisting on this formal repudiation of the 1975 resolution.

In retrospect, the General Assembly had made a serious mistake by equating Israel with Zionism. It should have realized that Zionism is a political project devised by Jews in Europe at the end of the nineteenth century, and while responsible for the world movement that successfully established Israel against great odds, it does not represent the Jewish people as whole, nor is it an authoritative expression of Judaism whether conceived as a religion or an ethno-historic tradition. From the inception of Zionism, Jews as individuals held wildly divergent, even contradictory, views about the wisdom of Zionism in theory and practice as well as about the validity of its relations with Judaism. Zionism was never institutionalized as the governing ideology of the Israeli state, and many Jewish critics of Israel emphasized the failure of the state to live up to either Zionist ideals or Judaic traditions.

Among the most fundamental of these disagreements related to whether Jews should aspire to a state of their own in Palestine, or should limit themselves to the Balfour pledge of support for a homeland in historic Palestine as delimited by the British mandate. The whole idea of an ethnic state is problematic given the geographic and demographic intermingling of ethnicities, and can be reconciled with the ideal of protecting the human rights of every individual only by artifice. In practice, an ethnic state, even if its activities are constitutionally constrained, dominates the governing space and discriminates against those with other ethnic identities. And so has been the case with Israel despite Palestinian voting rights and participation in the Knesset. Again, Zionism championed Israeli statehood as the fulfillment of the vision of a Jewish homeland, but the state that emerged is a political actor whose behavior needs to be appraised by its policies and practices, and not by its founding ideology.

Such general speculation raises somewhat different issues than are posed by the anti-Zionist resolution. Now the much more difficult issue is raised in the form of allegations that Israel as of 2016 has become a racist or apartheid state, most clearly with respect to its oppressive and discriminatory administration of the West Bank and Gaza. To be clear, it is not Zionism as an ideology that should be evaluated as racist or not, despite its ethnic exclusivity, but Israel as a state subject to international law, including the International Convention on the Elimination of Racial Discrimination (1966) and the International Convention on Suppression and Punishment of the Crime of Apartheid (1973).

BDS as Anti-Semitism?

At this time, complaints about anti-Semitism have taken an entirely different course, although emanating from a similar source. Instead of deflecting criticism at the UN by angry claims of institutional bias verging on anti-Semitism, Israel is now actually invoking the prestige of the UN to carry on its fight against the BDS Campaign and an alleged delegitimation project aimed at discrediting and isolating, if not destroying, the State of Israel. On May 31, 2016, Israel convened a day-long conference under the willfully misleading title, "Ambassadors Against BDS—International Summit at the UN." Invited speakers were limited to pro-Israeli extremists who took turns deploring BDS as a political initiative and denouncing its activist supporters as vicious anti-Semites. The Israeli ambassador, acting as convener of the conference and previously known mainly as an inflammatory leader of the settlement movement, Dani Danon, set the tone of the event with these words: "BDS is the modern incarnation of anti-Semitism," spreading an "ideology of hate."

The program was unabashedly one sided. The conference was sponsored by a series of leading Jewish organizations. The audience consisted of more than 1,500 invited guests who possessed strong anti-BDS credentials and who were encouraged to be militant in their opposition to BDS activities. The conference call relied on language that highlights the political significance of this extraordinary initiative. The BDS campaign continues to make strides in their campaign to delegitimize the State of Israel, stimulating Israel to mount its own anti-BDS campaign. They are gaining increased support on university campuses around the world, as well as some church groups and labor unions, as they promote initiatives on local and national levels calling to divest and boycott the Jewish state.[2] Such a statement accurately recognizes that BDS has become the main vehicle of a rapidly strengthening global solidarity movement that aligns itself with the Palestinian national movement, is effectively mobilizing beneath the BDS banner, and has been shaped since its inception in 2005 when it was endorsed by 170 Palestinian NGOs and a wide spectrum of civil society activists.

It should be clarified that the so-called anti-BDS "summit," appearances not withstanding, was not a UN conference, nor did it have the blessings or participation of top UN officials. It was an event organized by the Israeli delegation at the UN that was allowed to make use of UN facilities. Calling itself "Ambassadors Against BDS" is deceptive, suggesting some kind of collective diplomatic undertaking by the international community or at least its Western segment.

Contrariwise, and more to the point, several European governments normally supportive of Israel, including Sweden, Ireland, and even the Netherlands have recently officially indicated that support for BDS is a legitimate political activity, entitled to the protection of law in a democratic state, and its supporters should be treated as exercising their right to freedom of expression in a lawful manner.

The BDS goals are set forth clearly in its founding document and do not include the delegitimation of Israel *as a state*: (1) withdrawal of Israel forces from Arab territories occupied in 1967, including the Syrian Golan Heights as well as West Bank, Jerusalem, and Gaza; (2) respect for the right of return of Palestinian refugees in accordance with General Assembly Resolution 194; and (3) protection of the human rights of Palestinians living in pre-1967 Israel on the basis of full equality. Without question the BDS movement endorses an ambitious program, but it does not question Israeli sovereignty over pre-1967 Israel, despite its territorial control of 78 percent of the original Palestine Mandate, which is far more than what the UN considered fair in 1947 when it allocated about 45 percent of the territory to the Palestinians, and was rejected by the Palestinians as being grossly unfair given the demographics at the time, and considering that their connection with the land was based on long-term residence.

In a growing reaction to the growing influence of BDS, Israel and pro-Israeli civil society actors have been pushing back in a variety of settings with tactics that violate the written and unwritten rules of democratic society. Among the most salient of these tactics have been the successful efforts of the organized Jewish community in Britain to have an academic conference at Southampton University canceled for two consecutive years, the frantic defamatory assault on Penny Green, the distinguished British criminalist who had been proposed as the first choice of the selection committee in 2016 to be the new UN Special Rapporteur for Human Rights in Occupied Palestine, a travel ban imposed by Israel on Omar Barghouti, the widely admired worldwide leader of BDS, and sundry outrageous efforts throughout the United States to have as many state legislatures as possible pass punitive laws that defame BDS by associating its advocacy and activity with anti-Semitism.

Above all, this ugly effort to stigmatize BDS represents a double shift in the essential battlefield of the Israel–Palestine struggle. The first shift is from armed struggle to a series of symbolic encounters concerning the legitimacy of Israel's policies and practices. The second interrelated shift is away from inter-governmental diplomacy and toward civil society militancy. It is possible that the second shift is temporary or provisional, having as its objective the revival of normal diplomacy at a future time under conditions where both sides are treated equally, and the process facilitated by a genuinely neutral intermediary. In effect, an authentic peace process in the future must correct the flaws that doomed the diplomacy undertaken within the Oslo Framework of Principles to failure, and what is worse, operated to enable a steady dynamic of Israeli expansionism at Palestinian expense. One way of thinking of BDS is as a corrective to this failed diplomacy of the past.

In the meantime, both Israel and its civil society adversaries will reflect their contradictory agendas with respect to a variety of struggles centering on what should be deemed legitimate.

In important respects, the double shift should be welcomed. The BDS Campaign concentrates its efforts on university campuses, churches, and labor unions, and in relation to corporate and financial connections. To challenge the legality and propriety of its tactics is to attack the most fundamental values of constitutional democracy. BDS-bashing also lends indirect credibility to those who argue that only political violence can achieve justice for the Palestinian people by ending their unspeakable ordeal. It is reasonable, of course, to question whether BDS is effective, or to argue over its proper scope and tactics, but attacks on BDS as a valid political instrument should be repudiated.

Comparing Anti-Zionism in 1975 and Anti-BDS in 2016

This deadly dance between Zionism and the UN has now come full circle. In the 1970s, Zionism was condemned by the General

Assembly at the UN, and the condemnation was sharply criticized by Israel as being so anti-Semitic as to contaminate the Organization as a whole. In 2016, Israel in a dramatic turnabout relies on the stature and access associated with its UN membership to empower Zionist forces throughout the world to engage in BDS-bashing. In the end, we should appreciate that neither Zionism nor BDS are racist as such, and any serious inquiry should be directed at the behavior of Israel as a member of the UN obliged to respect international law and in relation to the actual claims and initiatives of BDS as a transnational civil society initiative seeking the implementation of international law and fundamental human rights.

It was a mistake to play the anti-Zionist card in 1975 as the real grievances of Palestinians and the UN were obscured behind the smokescreen of a false debate about whether or not deep criticisms of Israel were anti-Semitic. It is an even bigger mistake to play the anti-Semitic card in the current global setting as a way of evading the reasonable demands set forth by the BDS campaign, which seem on the face of it in accord with international law and morality, and have as a principal virtue the clear commitment to pursue political ends by peaceful means.

The scale of this mistake is enlarged by blurring the boundaries between a proper concern with anti-Semitism as a virulent form of ethnic hatred that has given rise in the past to bloody persecutions and fascist extremism, and most abhorrently to the Holocaust. Opposing BDS on its pragmatic or normative merits is an entirely reasonable posture for those who disagree with its premises, methods, and goals. What is not acceptable is to engage in these provocative and defamatory initiatives that seek to discredit and punish the proponents of BDS, and to threaten adherents with punitive pushback as happens when faculty tenure is abrogated or threatened and steps are taken to brand student activists by name as targets for vilification and intimidation.

The US State Department, the Definition of Anti-Semitism, and Edward Said's Humanism

Points of Departure

Four overlapping issues are addressed in the following analysis: first, the most dedicated supporters of Israel in Europe and North America have long tried to conflate criticism of Israel and Zionism with hatred of Jews, the traditional understanding of anti-Semitism, but this effort has intensified recently, and even has been endorsed by the US Government and is currently under consideration by the University of California and elsewhere; second, to examine the definition of anti-Semitism adopted by the US State Department, and discuss briefly why it has pernicious implications for academic freedom, and interferes with a genuine appreciation of the true nature and menace of anti-Semitism; third, to show why Edward Said, despite his intense opposition to anti-Semitism, would nevertheless be vulnerable to allegations of being an anti-Semite if the State Department definition were to be applied to his writings and activities; and fourth and finally to point out that, according to the imperatives most influentially expressed by Noam Chomsky and Said, the "responsibility of the intellectual" would perversely require them to be "anti-Semitic" according to this misleading conception now an expression of formal US policy.[1]

My personal awareness and understanding of this treacherous theme of anti-Semitism and Israel can be summarized by recalling two experiences. The first was in Greek Cyprus more than a decade ago at a session of the InterAction Council (composed of ex-heads of states) devoted to conflict resolution in the Middle East. I had been invited to participate as a resource person. During a discussion devoted to Israel/Palestine the Israeli ambassador to Greece spoke at some length, insisting that it was anti-Semitic to express strong criticisms of either Israel or Zionism, which in his presentation were indistinguishable. As the only other Jew at the table of political notables, I felt it to be almost a duty to clarify what I believed to be a mischievous manipulation of ideas. In my intervention I explained that Zionism was a project or ideology, Israel was a state, and that Jews were a people or an internationally dispersed collectivity of persons. I attempted to explain that to disagree with Zionism or to criticize Israeli policies and practices as a state should not be presupposed to be anti-Semitic, that anti-Semitism was expressed by exhibiting hostility, hatred, and discrimination against Jews as a people or as individuals. Recall that Hitler did not persecute Jews for being Zionists, but for being Jews, for their identity as a race or ethnicity. After the meeting recessed, several participants thanked me for my comments, indicating that only a Jew could offer this kind of clarification, which they found persuasive. In contrast, the Israeli ambassador and his NGO sidekick came to me to complain vigorously, insisting that Zionism had become synonymous with Jewish identity through the establishment of Israel as a state of the Jewish people, making the three ideas interchangeable. In effect, their separation was now deemed deeply hostile to the Jewish experience, and was properly viewed as "anti-Semitism." I walked away unconvinced by the conversation, yet disturbed by the tenor of the encounter, especially by their aggressive and condescending manner.

This trivial incident still seems relevant as it illustrates what I believe has been an effective effort by unconditional Israel supporters to stifle criticism of Israel by inappropriately deploying this charge of anti-Semitism. It is inappropriate as it merges what might be called genuine hate speech with an attempt to intimidate freedom of expression in a domain where it seems needed, that is, in the justifiable questioning of Israel's state behavior and the colonial nature of the Zionist project as it is playing out in the twenty-first century at the expense of the Palestinian people. It is a doubly unfortunate and dangerous tactic as it tends to weaken and confuse opposition to genuine anti-Semitism by insisting upon this misleading linkage of a contentious political argument with a condemnation of racism.

My second experience was to receive an email at the end of 2013 informing me that the Simon Wiesenthal Center in Los Angeles, a non-governmental organization known for its unconditional support of Israel, had issued its annual list of the ten most dangerous anti-Semites in the world, and that I was listed as third. I found it quite astounding, especially after discovering that #1 was the Supreme Guide of Iran and #2 was the then Prime Minister of Turkey. Others on the list included such notable authors as Alice Walker and Max Blumenthal. It was obvious that I was placed on the list as a consequence of my role as UN Special Rapporteur for Occupied Palestine in the period between 2008 and 2014. In the fulfillment of this role, I had indeed written very critically from the perspective of human rights and international law about the manner in which Israel was administering the occupation, which involved elements of annexation, ethnic cleansing, and apartheid. But nothing in my reports directly or indirectly exhibited hatred or hostility toward the Jewish people or toward Jews as Jews. My prominence on the Wiesenthal list at first troubled me deeply, fearing that it would damage my credibility as well as be a painful and unjustified attack on my Jewish identity that would be humiliating and probably ineffective to oppose. I never overcame these feelings, but they became somewhat offset by a realization that highlighting my name in this way could only be explained by the degree to which my UN reports were exerting some influence on the way in which the Israel–Palestine conflict was being more generally perceived and understood, especially within UN circles. I continue to feel a certain pride in bearing witness honestly, reporting the realities under law of Israel's occupation policies and practices, and emphasizing the extent to which prolonged Palestinian suffering and a collective experience of rightlessness and extreme vulnerability has been the result.

These personal recollections relate to the current debate nationally, internationally, and in California where I reside. The essential argument is that Jews in Europe feel threatened by what they describe as a new wave of anti-Semitism, which is deliberately linked to the rise of anti-Israeli activism, and was dramatized by several recent terrorist incidents, especially the 2014 parallel attacks on the French magazine *Charlie Hebdo* and a kosher supermarket in Paris. The European migration crisis is undoubtedly giving rise in Europe to a strengthening of the political right extreme, including its neo-Nazi fringe that does express real racial hatred properly identified as anti-Semitism, but it is far less currently virulent in its racism toward Jews than toward Muslims. One problem arising from this preoccupation with anti-Semitism is to treat Jews as accorded extra protection while at the same time immunizing hostility to Islam by reference to freedom of expression. There is no doubt that *Charlie Hebdo*, while victimized for its opinions, was disseminating with respect to Muslims the kind of hate images and messages that if directed at Jews would be properly regarded by almost everyone as anti-Semitism, including by myself.

It is somewhat understandable that Europe would be sensitive to a renewed presence of anti-Semitism, given that it was both the scene of the Holocaust, the historic center of anti-Semitism, and in many ways provided the historic vindication of the Zionist movement. We should not forget that the international validation of the Zionist quest for a Jewish homeland received its first formal encouragement in the notoriously colonialist letter written by the British Foreign Secretary, Lord Alfred Balfour, in 1917. As well, during the 1930s, prior to Hitler's adoption of the Final Solution, the preferred German and anti-Semitic solution of the so-called Jewish Problem in Europe was to exert intense pressure on Jews to emigrate to Palestine or even to be victimized by forced expulsion, and this was not solely a consequence of Nazi policies, but reflected anti-Semitic policies pursued in East Europe. Timothy Snyder in his important and authoritative book, *Black Earth*, documents the extent to which especially Polish anti-Semitic political leaders collaborated with Zionist leaders, including even providing military training and weapons that developed the Zionist militias that later were to challenge violently the British mandatory presence in Palestine and then successfully wage a war of independence against the indigenous Palestinian population and neighboring Arab states.[2] In effect, many European anti-Semites, who were prominent throughout the continent, shared with the Zionist leadership the belief that the way to solve "the Jewish problem" was to support the establishment of a Jewish homeland in Palestine, and in keeping with the prevailing colonial mentality gave little thought to the impact of such a development on the indigenous Arab population of Palestine.

The contemporary American argument and debate has less historical baggage compared to Europe and is more subtle, mainly focused on campus activity and is a reflection to some extent of the US government's "special relationship" with Israel. It is evident that Israeli officials definitely project the view that hostility to Israel or Zionism is indistinguishable from what the State Department calls "traditional anti-Semitism," that is, hatred or persecution of Jews because of their ethnicity. What is most troublesome in the State Department approach is its incorporation of what it calls "new anti-Semitism," which "manifests itself in the guise of opposition to Zionism and the existence and/or policies of the state of Israel." This "new anti-Semitism, characterized by anti-Zionist and anti-Israel criticism that is anti-Semitic in effect—whether or not in intent—[and] is more subtle and thus frequently escapes condemnation."[3]

The Board of Regents of the University of California is currently considering whether to adopt such a conception of anti-Semitism as official university policy. The principal arguments advanced in its favor are that pro-Palestinian student activism, especially around calls for boycotts and divestments, are making Jewish students feel uncomfortable, even under threat, with the further implication that such insecurity should not be present in any academic community. This rationale skirts the issue that the BDS campaign has been gaining significant traction in recent years, and this effort to brand the activist dimension of solidarity with the Palestinian struggle as anti-Semitic is motivated by a major multi-pronged Israeli effort to weaken BDS by having those who support such a campaign damaging to Israel be discredited by being found guilty of "anti-Semitism."

These developments recall my experience in Cyprus, and reflect this determined effort to meet the rise of Palestinian solidarity efforts with its suppression being justified as opposition to the new anti-Semitism. Also, to the same effect is Michael Oren's best-selling *Ally: My Journey Across the American–Israeli Divide*, a memoir depicting Israel's former ambassador to the US, describing his concerted efforts to render unacceptable any public utterance of criticism of Israel.[4] Note the features of this negative branding: only the sensitivities of Jews are singled out despite the far greater discomfort confronting Muslim minority students and others on campuses and throughout America; the initiative is overtly designed to weaken popular support for a just and sustainable peace in Palestine, given the collapse of diplomatic efforts to produce the two-state solution; the BDS campaign is being challenged in ways that never occurred during earlier comparable campaigns, especially in the American civil rights movement and the BDS movement contra South African apartheid, both of which strongly advocated boycott and divestment tactics, especially in contexts of universities, churches, and labor unions. Part of the broader context that is rarely mentioned in debating the proper scope of anti-Semitism is the degree to which a surge of pro-Palestinian nonviolent militancy has emerged in reaction to two developments: Israel's reliance on excessive force, collective punishment, and the persistence of such unlawful activities as settlement expansion; and the completion of the separation wall.

It is in this atmosphere of endowing smears of anti-Semitism with respectability that has become threatening to academic freedom in the manner of Cold War McCarthyism. The revocation of a tenure contract issued to Steven Salaita by the University of Illinois rested on the thin rationale that, because he had written several allegedly inflammatory tweets highly critical of Israel during Israel's 2014 attack on Gaza, he would bring bias into the classroom and make many of his students uncomfortable. In fact, Salaita possesses an outstanding performance record in the classroom at his previous university position at Virginia Tech. His teaching was greatly appreciated by his students, including those who were Jewish and pro-Israeli. Undoubtedly more serious than the high-profile cases are the invisible effects of this politically motivated and aggressive use of anti-Semitism, exhibited by a reluctance to hire or promote individuals who have engaged in Palestinian solidarity activity or even to invite speakers that would be subjected to criticism of bringing an anti-Semite accusations to campus.

Again my experience is unfortunately relevant. During the six years that I held the UN position, everywhere I went to speak, including at my former university, Princeton, or in foreign settings as remote as Beirut or Sydney, Australia concerted campaigns were organized by local and international Zionist groups to persuade the university administration to cancel my lectures. The claim being made was that I should not be allowed to speak because I was a notorious anti-Semite. These efforts were backed up by threats to withhold contributions to the university if the event went ahead as scheduled. These efforts failed, and my talks went ahead as scheduled without incident, but what the campaign did accomplish was to shift media and audience attention from the substance of my presentation to the utterly false issue of whether or not I was an anti-Semite, which of course, required me to deal with accusations that were hurtful as well as completely erroneous, and truly malicious.

Contra Anti-Semitism

It is against this background that I wanted to mention Edward Said's humanism, which in the context of this State Department approach, would clearly qualify as an unacceptable, if disguised, form of the "new anti-Semitism." It hardly needs mentioning that Edward Said was and in many ways remains the most passionate and influential voice of the Palestinian people, and indeed of people worldwide seeking liberation. His books, *Orientalism* and *Culture and Imperialism* continue to be read all over the world more than a decade after his death. I was privileged to have Edward Said as a close and cherished friend who over the years nurtured my interest in and engagement with the Israel–Palestine conflict, and whose remarkable life remains an inspiration for many who aspire to be public intellectuals. His views are peculiarly relevant to the theme of this chapter as he was both a fierce opponent of the old anti-Semitism and an exemplary exponent of "the new anti-Semitism," which as I insist should never be considered anti-Semitism at all. These organized attempts to discredit criticisms of Israel and Zionism should themselves be discredited, especially in view of their recourse to defamatory behavior and encouragement of witch-hunts that are newly endangering academic freedom.

As Said's colleague and close friend at Columbia University, Akeel Bilgrami, a distinguished professor of comparative literature observed, Said "despised anti-Semitism as much anyone I know."[5] Humanism was the only -ism with which Said was comfortable. His circle of identification extended far beyond his affirmation of Palestinian identity, embracing the human species as a whole, although rooted in the fierce particularity of his Palestinian heritage. His academic training, publications, and career were situated firmly in literature until awakened by the 1967 Six-Day War to take up the Palestinian struggle in a dedicated and public manner for the rest of his life.

Said's writing on Palestine was always informed by evidence and shaped by his deep grasp of history and culture, initially in his important *The Question of Palestine.*[6] What is striking about Said's approach, despite his righteous anger over the refusal of the world to appreciate and correct the terrible injustices done to the Palestinian people in the course of establishing and legitimating the Israeli state, is his steadfast appreciation that Zionism did what it did beneath the shadow of Nazi persecution, especially culminating in the Holocaust. In other words, his sense of the conflict with Israel is conceived in inclusive terms as pertaining to Jews as well as Palestinians. In his words,

> I have spent a great deal of my life during the past thirty-five years advocating the rights of the Palestinian people to national self-determination, but I have always tried to do that with full attention to the reality of the Jewish people, and what they suffered by way persecution and genocide.[7]

He never endorsed a solution to the struggle that was not sensitive to both Palestinians and Jews, and in a sense his approach embodied a principled rejection of the Israeli claim that the Palestinians were intent on pushing the Jews into the sea.

While insisting that Jews must never experience in Israel the sort of dispossession inflicted upon the Palestinian people by the Zionist project, Said was unrelenting in linking a sustainable peace to acknowledging the justices of the past. As he expressed it to Ari Shavit in one of his last interviews, "[U]ntil the time comes when Israel assumes moral responsibility for what it has done to the Palestinian people, there can be no end to the conflict." He goes on to add, "[W]hat is needed is a 'bill of particulars' of all our claims against Israel for the original dispossession and for the occupation that began in 1967."[8]

In effect, the injustices of the past can be superseded, but only if they are acknowledged in an appropriate format with due solemnity. On at least one occasion Said seems to suggest one possible mechanism would be a truth and reconciliation process modeled on what was done in South Africa after the fall of apartheid.

Said's central contribution of developing a critique of West-centric views of the Arab world are most influentially set forth in *Orientalism*, one of the most widely studied and seminal books of the past century. Among many other facets of the analysis in the book, it led Said to offer this surprising convergence: "Not accidentally, I indicate that Orientalism and modern anti-Semitism have common roots."[9] This

convergence is explained by the dual effort to achieve "a better understanding of the way cultural domination have operated."[10]

At the same time, Said felt that Zionist exclusivism sought to keep
the issue as limited to what Jews had endured in the Holocaust, which
could operate as a sufficient vindication of Zionism and the creation
of Israel, with the adverse effects on the Palestinians as self-inflicted
or irrelevant to this hegemonic Israeli narrative. Said writes that "all
liberals and even most 'radicals' have been unable to overcome the
Zionist habit of equating anti-Zionism with anti-Semitism." Long
before the present debate he believed that such an *informal* tactic
prevented truthful conversation as non-Jews were inhibited by "the
fear of treading upon the highly sensitive terrain of what Jews did to
their victims, in an age of genocidal extermination of Jews—all this
contributes to the dulling, regulated enforcement of almost unanimous
support for Israel."[11] Writing in the late 1970s, Said felt that Palestinian
criticisms of Israel were often insensitive to the background of its
establishment as a last bastion of defense for the Jewish people after the
ordeal of the Holocaust.

Almost 40 years later the context has altered, but not the effect
of treating anti-Zionism as anti-Semitism. Because of the failure to
establish some kind of solution, and given Israeli defiance of international law through the settlements, separation wall, reliance on
excessive force and collective punishment, the issue of injustice to the
Palestinians has captured the moral imagination of many people around
the world, especially students. As a result the Palestinian struggle has
become the leading unresolved morally symbolic struggle of our time,
a successor to the South African struggle against apartheid a generation
earlier. This understanding has been acknowledged at various times
by Nelson Mandela and Archbishop Desmond Tutu. Now the US
government itself intrudes its influence on American society to make
sure that the extended definition of anti-Semitism as incorporating
strong criticism of Israel and Zionism is treated as hate speech. This is
not only threatening freedom of expression and academic freedom, it
is eroding the capacity of American citizens to fight nonviolently for
what they believe is right in the world. When the government adopts
punitive measures to discourage the BDS campaign or even academic
conferences addressing the conflict, it is behaving in a profoundly
anti-democratic manner. Such behavior follows directly from the

understanding given to the "special relationship" binding Israel to the United States in a manner that often contradicts proclaimed national values and even national interests. Our former Secretary of State, John Kerry, boasted of the hundreds of occasions on which the USA has blocked votes critical of Israel within the UN System, without even bothering to consider whether any of these initiatives were substantively justified or not.

Bearing Truthful Witness

Finally, it is helpful to inquire why this debate about what is and what is not anti-Semitism relates to the responsibility of the public intellectual as this political presence has been interpreted, especially by Edward Said and Noam Chomsky. In his 2003 Preface to *Orientalism*, Said writes these telling words: "Above all, critical thought does not submit to state power or to commands to join in the ranks marching against one or another approved enemy."[12] Frequently, Said reinforces the role of the intellectual to remain on the margins, an outsider, whose only weapon is bearing witness and truth-telling, a role authenticated by the absence of any claim to have a scholar's expert knowledge, more a standing in solidarity with those being victimized by oppression and injustice, a normative posture that rests on moral and legal foundations of respect for the value of all persons and peoples. Said's succinct expression is memorable. He characterizes the public intellectual "as exile and marginal, as amateur, and as the author of a language that tries to speak truth to power."[13]

The irony of this orientation of the intellectual is that it collides directly with the State Department conception of the new anti-Semitism. In other words, to avoid the blanket charge of anti-Semitism as now officially defined Said would have to renounce his chosen identity as a public intellectual. This would weaken the quality of academic freedom as well as undermine public discourse. No resource of higher education is more precious, in my judgment, than the presence of those all too few public intellectuals who challenge the prevailing wisdom of the society on the basis of conscience and truthfulness. It is the foundation of vigilant citizenship, early in the history of the republic recognized by Thomas Jefferson as indispensable for sustaining democracy, and it is also the basis for challenging vested interests and mistaken policies.

This role of public intellectuals is threatened by this assault on freedom of expression wrapped up in a false effort to discourage anti-Semitism, and it relates to such broader concerns as the stifling of political discourse due to the corporatization of the media and higher education.

On no issue is this unfettered dialogue more needed in the United States than in relation to Israel–Palestine. As Michael Oren argues repeatedly throughout his memoir *Ally*, the special relationship bonding Israel and the United States implies the absence of any public acknowledgement of policy disagreements and a policy of unconditional support. Israel did its bit to uphold its end of this unseemly bargain recently by being the only country of 194 in the UN that supported the United States' determination to maintain sanctions on Cuba, despite Obama's welcome decision to renew diplomatic relations. After all American taxpayers have long sent annually billions of dollars to Israel, as well as a range of weapons and munitions. They are entitled to know if this money is being spent in a manner that accords with international law and American national interests. The political costs of overriding Israel's objections to the Iran Nuclear Agreement illustrated the extent to which Israel can mount a formidable challenge to vital policy initiatives undertaken by the elected leaders of the American government.

Never have we more needed to protect and celebrate our public intellectuals, and never more so than in the context of Israel–Palestine. For this reason we should be celebrating the legacy of Edward Said, a world famous public intellectual, and the person, who more than anyone on the planet, fulfilled the role of responsible public intellectual. Instead of defending him against hypothetical incendiary charges of anti-Semitism, we should be honoring his memory by studying his ideas and enacting the values of resistance and struggle that he commends in the face of injustice.

Exposing Israel's True Quest

In concluding, there is an obvious tension that exists more vividly than when Edward Said was alive, and was commenting often and influentially on the Palestinian struggle. Israel has created on the ground a set of circumstances that seem irreversible and are institutionalizing a single apartheid Israeli state encompassing the whole of historic

Palestine as defined by the British Mandate. The Israeli leadership has made increasingly clear its opposition to establishing a Palestinian state, and given the insistence on making even the Palestinians acknowledge Israel as "a Jewish state," the die seems cast. At the same time, the international Palestinian solidarity movement has never been stronger, with the BDS campaign leading the way, moving from success to success. And so "the battlefield" has shifted to a Legitimacy War that the Palestinians are mostly winning. Israel has responded to these new threats with an all-out effort to demonize as anti-Semitism non-violent resistance and global solidarity initiatives. This is the essential objective of the idea of the new anti-Semitism, and it is scandalous that the US State Department, and implicitly the entire US Government, has endorsed such demonization with its newly adopted formal definition of anti-Semitism. To defeat this effort is essential not only for the Palestinian struggle, but to keep America safe for democratic discourse and universities hospitable to the kind of critical thinking that Edward Said's scholarship and activism so vividly exemplified.

PART IV

EDWARD SAID'S VOICE AND LEGACY

I 2

The Failed Peace Process: A Prophetic Indictment

The aim of this chapter is to consider Edward Said's perspective on Palestine's struggle for a just solution as continuing to provide the clearest and most thoughtful assessments despite his departure from the scene over a decade ago. I also consider what would be his likely approach to the present challenges facing the Palestinian people. The first part of this exercise depicts Said's approach, and the second my sense of the existing reconfiguration of the conflict in its post-Oslo phase.

I have the impression that despite Said's celebrity as Palestine's most influential public intellectual, there was not a widespread appreciation of the complex, evolving, and inclusive nature of his views on what is to be done, given the realities of Israel's existence and Palestine's ordeal, as well as the dynamics of the conflict itself. It is helpful to realize that Said was "born twice" (in Elias Khoury's phrase), once from his mother's womb in 1935, and a second time in the psychological incubator of anger and alienation that followed the outcome of the 1967 War.[1] It is intriguing to observe that this military victory achieved by Israel in 1967 had such contradictory effects—on the strategic side, converting previously hesitant US bureaucrats in the State Department and Pentagon into true believers in Israel's true worth as a partner in the region while pushing previously politically aloof Palestinian intellectuals onto the playing field of the conflict as ardent supporters of the national struggle.

There is a preliminary caveat about undertaking this assessment that should be addressed openly. Palestinians have been harmed over the decades by the supposed benevolent initiatives of non-Palestinians deliberating and making decisions from vantage points geographically and psychologically external to Palestine itself. Whenever a non-Palestinian comments upon the Palestinian failure to overcome their misery after decades of struggle, there should always be an accompanying note of humility. The Palestinian ordeal has been repeatedly shaped by political forces external to Palestine delimiting conceptions of what supposedly serves the common good. Until 1948, these external actors had the means to implement their ideas with tragic consequences for the Palestinians. It is well to recall that the whole political drama that has unfolded over the past century was highlighted by such global happenings as the colonialist commitment to the Zionist movement contained in the Balfour Declaration, the League of Nations assignment of Britain to administer the mandate as a supposedly "sacred trust of civilization," the United Nations as the dumping ground for British frustrations with their mandatory role, the UN proposed partition of Palestine that accorded the Jewish minority, which was at the time, about 30 percent of the population, 55 percent of the territory, and not surprisingly was rejected by Palestinian leaders and neighboring Arab governments. What ensued, of course, was a war in 1948 that resulted in statehood and membership in the UN for Israel, dispossession and dispersal of the Palestinians, with a much constrained territorial presence, which shrank to 22 percent in the 1948 War, and subsequently, considerably less due to the ever expanding settlements and their territorially encroaching infrastructure.

Against this background two conclusions can be reasonably drawn. First, Palestinians have been severely victimized by these past international decisions affecting Palestine that were reached with stunning disregard of the rights and well-being of the indigenous population; second, that it is integral to the right of self-determination that its practical implementation be exercised by the "self," in this instance by the Palestinians, and not by any supposed benefactor acting on their behalf. The Palestinian people have the discretion to freely exercise this right so long as it doesn't encroach upon the rights of others. Of course, there are severe current difficulties about whether any political actor is now available to speak authoritatively and legitimately represent the grievances and aspirations of the Palestinian people. What is clear to me, and was crystal clear to Said, is that neither Washington nor Tel Aviv had any entitlement to impose their views or even to hand the Palestinians a set of proposals on a take it or leave it basis, which seemed to be the dominant motif of past diplomatic efforts to find a solution by means of direct negotiations of the sort carried on within the Oslo framework. In reality, it is more accurate to portray this Oslo experience as negotiations without negotiating. Even if the US Government was credible when claiming to be the honest mediator, which scholarly research challenges, the perception of partisan alignment should have disqualified it from playing the role of neutral intermediary. Surely, one aspect of the Palestinian tragedy, as early recognized by Said, was the strange mixture of naiveté on Yasir Arafat's part, trusting the good faith of the United States despite many indications to the contrary, and the weakness of the Palestinian international stature as exhibited in its inability to insist on what should have been an unchallenged premise of diplomatic credibility: neutral third-party mediation.

Edward Said's Approach to Palestine

The basic orientation of Said was clearly expressed in his Preface to the 1992 edition of *The Question of Palestine* when he wrote:

> the main aspects of Palestine life remain dispossession, exile, dispersion, disenfranchisement (under Israeli military occupation), and, by no means last, an extraordinarily widespread and stubborn resistance to these travails.[2]

Each of these words are organically related to Said's own tireless efforts to reflect upon the conflict and what to do about it, and not just from a Palestinian perspective. Unlike many partisans on both sides, Said's vision of the future was one that included a concern with justice for the Israelis and empathy for their historical narrative, especially taking notice of the enormity of the Holocaust as a defining catastrophic trauma experienced by the Jewish people centrally engaged in the Israeli experience. This feature of his outlook that his pro-Israeli critics never acknowledge, or conveniently overlook, is integral to Said's profound commitment to a universalizing humanism that encompasses ethnic and religious differences without erasing the particularities of national belonging and collective identities.

More than ten years after his death, Edward Said's approach to the Palestinian struggle seems more relevant and challenging than ever, more so than when he was alive because the two-state consensus that he came to deplore on both principled and pragmatic grounds now seems impossible of realization, even to many of its former champions. Twenty years ago there was a widespread, although misguided, acceptance of the two-state approach as a political breakthrough, creating for the first time what appeared to many to be the only practical path to a solution. Such an outlook was supposedly vindicated by the mutual acceptance of the Oslo Framework of Principles as memorialized by that famous handshake on the White House Lawn. Yitzhak Rabin's assassination two years later by an Israeli right-wing extremist suggested that there existed in Israel influential persons who believed that Oslo was a slippery slope toward genuine Palestinian statehood, which would shatter the maximalist Zionist dream that coveted the whole of biblical Palestine as the eventual Jewish state.

Prior to Oslo, even Said provisionally endorsed the Palestine National Council decision in 1988 that indicated a willingness to accept the Israel of 1967 in the event of a full Israeli withdrawal from the occupation and an acceptance of Palestinian sovereign statehood. Said quite correctly observed that this extraordinary unilateral readiness for conflict resolution on the part of the Palestinians was never reciprocated or even acknowledged in the West as a major unilateral attempt by Palestinians to find "peace" even at the sacrifice of basic Palestinian rights under international law. Such a Palestinian desire for peace and accommodation with Israel was even more impressive because prior to Oslo, the expression of Palestinian collective unity was grounded in the inclusive procedures of the Palestine National Council and the overall respect accorded Arafat's leadership of the PLO.

The two-state solution was based on the dual plausible occurrences of Israel's withdrawal to the 1967 borders with small negotiated adjustments in compliance with Security Council Resolution 242 and the ensuing establishment of Palestine as a fully sovereign state. It was from the outset a misguided vision as it was dependent on the implicit conviction that the refugee issue could be finessed, as well as striking a posture of ambiguity about the degree to which Israel would be allowed to retain its archipelago of unlawful settlements. Perhaps, its most corrosive feature was the one-sided preoccupation with satisfying Israeli security concerns that could only be met within a permanent structure of acute Palestinian insecurity and vulnerability as concretized by the demand of a demilitarized Palestine. Even such a critique of the two-state consensus so widely endorsed internationally at an inter-governmental level is undoubtedly too mild as there is little evidence that any Israeli leadership, or even the Israeli public, was ever genuinely committed to establishing a Palestinian state that enjoyed full sovereign rights and political independence on the basis of equality with Israel or involved the substantial dismantling of the settlements. The Israeli two-state narrative always had the built-in proviso of Palestinian permanent demilitarization, and hence inequality and subordination, if not subjugation. The overt justification for Israel's insistence on Palestinian demilitarization was its contention that since Israel was surrounded by hostile Arab neighbors it needed exceptionally firm security arrangements if it were to agree to the emergence of even a quasi-Palestinian state.

By now most of the more humane and dedicated advocates of a two-state approach admit that any cycle of revived negotiation is a road to nowhere, or maybe something worse. One of the most influential proponents of an approach to reconciliation based on diplomacy, Henry Siegman, the highly intelligent and respected Jewish leader, is dismissive of any further negotiations given the current political atmosphere. He persuasively contends that throughout Netanyahu's entire career he has opposed every step taken in the direction of peace with the Palestinians, and remains as committed as ever to an expansionist view of Israel's territorial boundaries. Siegman insists that Netanyahu has used negotiations instrumentally merely to divert attention and avoid international pressure.[3] The US Government well understands that Netanyahu has no intention of ever allowing a sovereign Palestinian state to come into existence, but cynically supports negotiations for his own domestic reasons and to maintain the illusion that "a peace process" exists.

Underneath Siegman's dismissal of Oslo diplomacy as a failure is a fundamental disagreement with Said's approach: Siegman endorses the idea of a democratic Jewish state provided it allows a Palestinian state to come into being, but on the basis of past frustrations with bilateral negotiations. Instead of persisting with diplomacy that has proved futile, Siegman favors a solution imposed by Washington, a treatment of the refugee issue in a manner that does not challenge the ethno-religious organization of Israel, and a forward-looking approach that seeks a measure of present justice and relief from the ordeal of occupation while refusing to take any account of the massive past injustices toward the Palestinians in the form of the *nakba* and what followed.[4] Such a solution, even granting that it is well-meant as a response to the frustrations of diplomacy, nevertheless seems unlikely to be either acceptable or desirable for several reasons: it circumvents the core Palestinian right of self-determination relying on a geopolitically implemented outcome that continues the process of making decisions about Palestine (and Israel) without the organic participation of Palestinians or Israelis; it seems also to marginalize that part of the Palestinian agenda dealing with dispossession and dispersion, reducing the peace bargain to one of "land for peace." Further, it makes no integral attempt to achieve peace and reconciliation of the two peoples by an acknowledgement of past Israeli crimes against humanity.[5]

Of course, in favor of the Siegman approach, are the following considerations: it allows the Zionist project to be maintained, and thus does not seek that facet of "the impossible"; it acknowledges the inability and unwillingness of the parties to agree on their own within the Oslo framework or one of their own devising; and it gives the Palestinians as much substantive satisfaction as they are likely to receive, including an end to the occupation, unlikely to be otherwise achieved, given the balance of forces and the continuing leverage exerted by realist diplomacy, which is premised upon bargaining on the basis of capabilities and what is actually possessed rather than upon legal and moral entitlements.

Said's critique addressed what he believed to be the fundamental flaws and shortcomings of the Oslo approach to the implementation of Security Council Resolution 242 as the road to peace, what came to be called during the Bush presidency as "The Roadmap." Said was unwilling to look forward to peace without first looking backward at the events of 1948, the *nakba*. He was insistent that a formal acknowledgement by Israel of its moral and political responsibility for the dispossession of several hundred thousand Palestinians in 1948, and for the resulting refugee and exile status of millions more of Palestinian descendants of those expelled are taken into account. This is an important aspect of Said's distinctive view of how to address and resolve the conflict. He was unwavering in an insistence upon the satisfaction of this psycho-political precondition for a sustainable peace. It is significant that Palestinian governmental leaders have never made such a negotiating demand, likely because its assertion would cause friction that would preclude even the nominal forms of diplomacy that have occurred from time to time. Israeli officials have never indicated a scintilla of readiness to offer the Palestinians an apology for the *nakba* or to admit formally any wrongdoing, and not even a public show of empathy for the catastrophe that befell the Palestinian people in 1948. Such a statement is not meant to overlook important revisionist writing on the Israeli side that does lament the cruelties of the dispossession, and acknowledge both the foundational injustices and those that followed over the years.

For Said, such an acknowledgement by Israel constitutes the moral foundation that must exist if a sustainable coexistence between Israelis and Palestinians is ever to become a realistic project. Said's words in 2000 in the course of an interview with Ari Shavit, the prominent *Haaretz* journalist and author of *Our Promised Land*, confirm this set of convictions: "Until the time comes when Israel assumes moral responsibility for what it has done to the Palestinian people, there can be no end to the conflict." He goes on to explain,

"What is needed at the very least, is an acknowledgement of the destruction of Palestinian society, of the dispossession of Palestinian people, and the confiscation of their land. And also the destruction and suffering of the last fifty-two years, including such actions as the killing at Sabra and Shatila refugee camps."[6]

Of course, there are other events that have occurred in the last ten years: Israel's defiance of the findings of the near unanimous World Court in 2004 that the "Separation Wall" built on occupied Palestine was unlawful, should be dismantled, and Palestinians compensated for harm experienced; the 2006 deliberate air attacks on residential neighborhoods in Beirut; the massive Operation Cast Lead of 2008–2009 that deliberately targeted civilians and non-military targets in Gaza; the violent destruction of the Mavi Marmara humanitarian mission in 2010; and the 2012 and 2014 massive military assaults on Gaza involved war crimes and crimes against humanity. If all of the Israeli wrongs from the perspective of law and morality were to be compiled, it would be a long list, and could perhaps be least disruptively addressed by a Truth and Reconciliation mechanism as a dimension of a genuine peace process.

This issue of acknowledgement has additional significance. It relates to whether there exists any current basis for negotiating a mutually acceptable solution by way of the diplomatic mechanisms that are available. It would seem that Israel as currently governed has not the slightest intention of offering an apology to the Palestinian people, and therefore we must either conclude that peace is presently non-negotiable or that Said was wrong to make this symbolic form of redress for historic grievances an unconditional precondition. If it is a precondition, why privilege only the physical dispossession from 1948 onwards, and not take any account of the earlier encouragement of dispossession by way of a colonialist edict of permission to the Zionist movement without any effort to consult the indigenous population? More recently, it is worth commenting upon the exchange in 2004 of letters between Ariel Sharon, then Israel's prime minister, and George W. Bush, that purported to reassure Israel that the United States would look with favor on Israel's territorial incorporation of settlement blocs although constructed unlawfully on occupied Palestinian territory. The implicit colonialist assumption is that this dismissal of Palestinian rights could be achieved without either the participation or a show of consent by the representatives of the Palestinian people. No one would deny that these letters have political weight despite lacking either moral or legal authority. In the end, the relevance of the letters will be determined by the overall context in which the struggle is finally brought to an end, whether happy or tragic.

Despite Said's insistence that the *nakba* and subsequent criminality by Israel operates as a precondition to a just and sustainable peace, his vision is not insensitive to the Jewish ordeal that gave rise and effectiveness to the Zionist project. It is notable that Said couples his rather strong demand for acknowledgement with a carefully reasoned rejection of any Palestinian insistence on the dispossession of the Jews living in Israel. In the interest of moving forward with minimum further suffering, Said overlooks the illegitimacy of the Zionist undertaking even while taking note that it was facilitated by colonial fiat in the form of the Balfour Declaration. In effect, for Said, Palestinian self-determination cannot be legitimately exercised by recourse to a second dispossession, this time victimizing the Jewish people even if it is established that their presence in Palestine was the outcome of an abusive colonial process since discredited. In this sense,

Said starkly refuses to perpetuate any further reproduction of injustice of the sort that was visited upon the Palestinians under the shadow of the massive criminality of the Nazi experience of persecution and genocide that had been such a profoundly traumatizing experience for the Jews of Europe. He wants to break the cycle whereby victims become victimizers. His vision of a just peace was stubbornly inclusive, premised on the "co-existence and equality" of these two tormented peoples, neither more nor less. In his words, "these are equal peoples and have to live together as communities each with their own sense of self."[7]

Said was unyielding as to what he regarded to be fundamentals of justice associated especially with unforgiveable wrongs done in the past and responsible for the suffering to varying degrees of all Palestinians, especially refugees, including those, like himself, who had built their lives in foreign lands: "I have no place. I'm cut off from my origins. I live in exile."[8] The wounds of the past remain, and can only be healed by the remorse of those who stand in the shoes of the perpetrators made tangible by an equal sharing of rights and territory.

Revisiting the Said Approach

There are some important changes in the past ten years that might alter Said's perspective. As indicated, the two-state approach, although still affirmed as the only path to peace by the international community and by relevant political leaders on both sides, increasingly lacks credibility. The rise of the radical right in Israel together with the passivity of Palestinian secular leadership in Ramallah has caused widespread disillusionment as to the role of traditional diplomacy in bringing the Palestinian ordeal to an end. It is also the case that Palestinian resistance efforts have shifted toward the adoption of nonviolent tactics and a greater reliance on a global solidarity movement. In effect, the Palestinians are waging and winning a Legitimacy War for control of the heights of international morality and international law, for the public perception of justice and right. Contrary to what governmental realists proclaim and rely upon at great human and material costs, the political outcome of most conflicts since 1945 (but not before) has been controlled by the winners of Legitimacy Wars and not by the side with hard power dominance. Putting this trend differently, international morality and international law are better predictors of who will prevail in conflicts than the balance of military forces. In almost every major encounter of recent decades, the eventual winner was the weaker side from the perspective of hard power, and the stronger side from the perspective of soft power. The successful struggle of the nonviolent Indian independence movement against the then mighty British Empire is paradigmatic of this trend, as is the success of the anti-apartheid campaign against the arrayed power of the racist elite in control of the South African state, or the victory of the Vietnamese against the United States. In effect, military superiority has lost much of its historical agency, even as it has geometrically increased its destructive ferocity and technological sophistication. The resulting human tragedy is that tens of millions of people have died and many societies devastated because the realist mentality that controls the foreign policy of most powerful states has yet to learn this lesson about the demilitarizing shift in the nature of power and historical agency.

A second element here involves a challenge to the other dimension of realism: its presumption that only what is presently perceived as "feasible" is attainable, building on the conventional wisdom that politics is the art of the possible. Again the historical record presents a more complicated picture that includes many outcomes in conflict situations that were viewed as impossible until after they happened: the bloodless collapse of the apartheid regime; the defeat of France and then the United States in the Indochina War; the liberation of the countries of Eastern Europe from oppressive regimes; the upheavals of 2011 in the Arab world. In other words, the impossible happens, and in situations where the demands of justice do not seem feasible, it becomes plausible to pursue what I have described elsewhere as "the politics of impossibility."

In effect, we are not smart enough to be pessimistic (or optimistic), and so what is socially and politically desirable and morally just should not be excluded from political programs because it seems presently "utopian," that is, not capable of being set forth in the form of a political project with a sequence that carries us from here to there. In this way of thinking, the impossible can quickly change its character. When I was in South Africa in the late 1960s, no one even dreamed that the

Afrikaaner leadership of the country would release Nelson Mandela from prison, and allow a relatively peaceful transition to a multi-racial constitutional democracy, and this continued to be so in the early 1990s. In other words, when the impossible happens it can occur with great suddenness, defying all expert expectations. And of course, the Zionist movement is itself a prime example of an "impossible" project being historically realized.

Putting the present circumstances surrounding the Israel–Palestine struggle into context, I would stress five political dimensions:

1. *The Politics of Dispossession, Encroachment, Confiscation*: Israel's continuing efforts to alter facts on the ground by moves toward annexation, ethnic cleansing, as well as establishing a form of quasi-permanent military administration based on systematic and severe discrimination that appears to constitute the crime of apartheid;

2. *The Politics of Deflection*: The Israeli effort to shift attention from the message to the messenger, blaming its negative international image on the biased and tainted UN auspices of critical inquiry; a range of initiatives that include: an exaggerated focus on an alleged threat by Iran; changing the conversation by claiming that Israel's behavior is over-scrutinized with respect to human rights as compared to other countries with far worse records;

3. *The Politics of Fragmentation*: multiple forms of fragmenting Palestinian unity with the intention of deconstructing and weakening Palestinian claims and grievances: Hamas v. Fatah; West Bank v. Gaza Strip; Separation Wall; erasing the Palestinian minority in Israel; ignoring the grievances of refugees and those living in exile;

4. *The Politics of Hard Power*: The interactions of violence as between the Occupied and the Occupier; state uses of force versus resistance based on armed struggle;

5. *The Politics of Soft Power*: The mobilization of transnational civil society; the struggle to control the heights of international morality and law; enlisting public opinion and viewing the UN as a series of sites of struggle; what Israelis deride as "lawfare" or "the delegiti-mation project," versus what I have called the "Legitimacy War." Israel, on its side, also relies on soft power to exert influence, taking

the principal form of elaborate efforts to create a positive international "brand Israel" and to deride its civil society opponents as anti-Semites.

Arguably, Israel dominates 1–4, while the Palestinians are winning only 5, the Legitimacy War, but this may turn out to be sufficient.

A Concluding Observation

I am not suggesting that the Palestinians can look forward to such a positive future, but I am saying that there is reason to believe that Palestine is winning the Legitimacy War, and that this could create a situation where surprising developments occur that recalibrate the balance of forces in favor of the Palestinians. In effect, I am suggesting that recent global trends in conflict resolution support the belief that history is being made by people and related solidarity movements rooted in civil society and reinforced by world public opinion, more than it is governments and diplomats, often at shocking costs in death and devastation. In Mahmoud Darwish's poem of farewell to Edward Said written several years ago, we find the following relevant lines:

He also said: If I die before you
my will is the impossible
I asked: is the impossible far off?

In the same poem, Darwish also wrote the words:

… We can
change the inevitability of the abyss.

And urged trust in:

the candor of the imagination.

I suppose from a more prosaic perspective I am trying to complement the vision of Edward Said with that of his poetic prophetic twin, Mahmoud Darwish. On this basis, I would encourage all of us to take responsibility for making the impossible possible when it comes to the pursuit of a just outcome for the peoples of Palestine and Israel. We must not be misled by accepting the (mis)guidance of self-proclaimed realists who continue to shape the policies of government, proclaiming that the achievement of justice and genuine peace is unattainable for the Palestinians, and indeed for the peoples of the entire Middle East. It is the task of citizens of conscience everywhere to think and act otherwise.

13

Palestine as a "Lost Cause"

This chapter is mainly a commentary upon Said's fascinating essay titled "On Lost Causes" that combines intriguing literary assessments with his complex understanding of the Palestinian ordeal and destiny.[1] This essay was one of his last major interpretative contributions, being the published form of a Tanner Lecture given at the University of Utah in 1997, and according to his friend and associate, Andrew Rubin, was regarded by Said as the publication that satisfied him most in this final period of his life.

Part of my interest in this theme of "lost causes" derives from a rather tense encounter I had with the French ambassador to the UN at a private dinner in New York City at the end of my term as UN Special Rapporteur for Occupied Palestine. Our host had invited a dozen or so diplomats who sat around the table to comment upon the Israel–Palestine conflict as they waited for the main course to be served, and I was expected to respond. This typically over-confident and somewhat belligerent French diplomat started the ball rolling with some very provocative statements: "Let's face it, the conflict is over, Israel has won, the Palestinians have been defeated, there is nothing more to be done or said. I am not happy about this, but this is the reality. We should move on." In effect, in the spirit of cynical realism, he was declaring that the Palestinian struggle was over, and although he acknowledged, this may be regrettable, it is time to move on. In a way, my choice of focus here can be seen as a more considered response to this French ambassador that evening, as an insistence on my part that Palestine is not a lost cause in his sense, and even if it were a lost cause from the perspective of realism, a continued commitment to the Palestinian struggle is greatly to be preferred to some kind of defeatist resignation and indifference toward such a grossly unjust outcome of such an epic struggle.

My deeper conviction is that the appearance of Palestinian defeat is an optical illusion that hides the deeper reality of a probable eventual Israeli defeat, that while Israel is winning one war due to its military dominance and continuous establishment of facts on the ground, Palestine is winning what in the end is the more important war, the legitimacy struggle that is most likely to determine the political outcome. If the outcome of international conflicts during the last 50 years is carefully considered, it reveals the astonishing conclusion that the weaker side militarily controlled the political outcome almost all of the time in struggles against *foreign* rule and occupation. It turns out that in recent history it is the side with the greater perseverance and resilience, not the side that controls the battlefield that wins in the end. This is a profound, and very new reality that was not true at all during the era of European colonialism, and not generally until 1945 at the end of World War II.

This failure of foreign intervention and occupation should have been the lesson that the US Government learned in Vietnam, but failed to do so. It remains the great unlearned anti-realist lesson: military superiority in this period unlike in early periods has lost most of its historical agency in politically and ethically oriented conflicts against *foreign, especially Western, domination*, although military superiority continues to shape the course of battlefield outcomes, but this no longer determines the outcome of wars. It was a lesson already captured by the extraordinary ending of Pontecorvo's 1966 film, *The Battle of Algiers*, in which the defeated Algerian movement of national liberation miraculously achieved its victory over French colonialism. As George W. Bush discovered in Iraq, it is possible for the Western intervener to win easily the first type of war, and yet go on to lose the vital legitimacy struggle that follows. In the end, the political goals that prompted the military attack in the first place lose their claim to be a "mission accomplished" and become acknowledged many deaths later as a "mission impossible."

Some years ago I lent emotional support to a Hawaiian native rights movement, and came to know its inspirational leader, Kekuni Blaisdell. Blaisdell, who was from a leading Hawaiian family, had become one of the first medical doctors in Honolulu with a conscious native heritage. He succeeded professionally in the Westernized world of modern Hawaii, more or less ignoring his own background or the degree to which traditional Hawaii was a casualty of American colonizing ambitions. In mid-life, Kekuni awakening to his previously ignored native identity, learned the Hawaiian language and its songs, dedicating himself to the small but determined Hawaiian independence movement and a celebration of the memory of the lost Hawaiian kingdom. Surely, this was the adoption of a lost cause, a contradictory life choice to that of an opportunist who jumps on the bandwagon so as to be situated on what realists would identify as the winning side. Yet Kekuni, in choosing to align with the lost cause of Hawaiian independence, became fulfilled in ways that far transcended his earlier professional success or the kind of life experience of Hawaiians who passively accepted the historical verdict of their defeat. Somehow his luminous dedication generated love and devotion to this man that was quite unrelated to the awareness that his vision of a restored Hawaii seemed doomed, surely a lost cause if ever there was one. He was enacting in life what Don Quixote exemplifies in literature.

In a similar vein, Said in his essay on lost causes refers to the Japanese veneration of "noble failure" as a superior course of action in life. His prime literary example happens to be Don Quixote, whose absurd mission to revive an ethos of chivalry, the noble knight's way of life in Spain was doomed to failure, yet who achieved notable personal success in the midst of mundane failure by embodying in his life a vision that was redemptive. In Said's words,

> Of course, the Don is unsuccessful in restoring Amadis of Gaul and [the] age of chivalry, but the strength of his conviction is such as even to expose the sordid reality of this extremely unheroic world of ours—with its innkeepers, shepherds, itinerant rogues—to an idealism whose self-conviction and fervor look backward to an age that has disappeared.[2]

This faith in the unrealizable achieves a fulfilling repudiation of what history has brought to pass even if the glorified past cannot be reclaimed.

Said is careful to distinguish cultural tropes in the domain of literary imagination from the flesh and blood realities of political struggle. Near the beginning of the long essay he identifies a lost cause as one: "associated in the mind and in practice with a hopeless cause: that is, something you support or believe in that can no longer be believed in except as something without hope of achievement." He goes on to say, "the cause and belief has passed, the cause no longer seems to contain any validity or promise, although it may once have possessed both." At that point, he poses what he calls "the crucial question," which is to decide whether such a judgment hinges on interpretation alone or is based on objective circumstances. In this respect, the lostness of a lost cause is itself problematized. Said happens also to refer to the example of pursuing Hawaiian independence, observing that what seems lost at the moment may become attainable at some future time when circumstances change, beyond our powers of anticipation, which they repeatedly do, although not invariably. Ironically, of course, this was the experience of the Zionist Project, which would have almost certainly have remained a lost cause without the drastically changed circumstances brought about by the Holocaust.

But there exists a contrary view that effectively denies the contingency of experience and places its trust in the reliability of appearances. The French diplomat expressed this attitude by being so sure that the Palestinians had been defeated once and for all. Said describes such an outlook as that of "a strict determinist about the survival only of powerful nations and peoples." In that case, as Said points out, "the cause of native rights in Hawaii, or gypsies or aborigines, is always necessarily a lost cause, something both predestined to lose out and because of belief in the overall narrative of power, required to lose."[3]

Before turning to the present phase of the Palestinian struggle, there is another general idea that relates closely to apparently lost causes that should lead to further reflection on lostness and failure. This additional line of thinking is suggested by the anti-realism of such seminal figures as Alain Badiou and Slavoj Žižek. In effect, they argue it is *only* lost causes that have the empowering potential to address the challenges confronting humanity. In this sense, abandoning the Enlightenment legacy of relying on the guidance of instrumental reason, Žižek proposes "a Leap of Faith," in his words, "[w]hat lies beyond involves a Leap of Faith, faith in lost causes, causes that from within the space of skeptical wisdom, cannot but appear as crazy."[4] It seems worth observing that at one stage Theordor Herzl, the founder of the modern Zionist movement, supposedly endorsed the early Zionist slogan, "you don't have to be crazy to be a Zionist, but it helps."

That is, a burning faith in the unrealizable creates the possibility, however remote, that what seems beyond reach will at some point be reached.

But why strike such a posture? Žižek's response, which I share and which is very different from the focused craziness proposed by Herzl, is expressed as follows:

> the problem, of course, is that in a time of crisis and ruptures, skeptical empirical wisdom itself, constrained to the horizons of the dominant form of common sense, cannot provide the answers, and so one must risk a leap of faith.[5]

Put more simply, that the realm of the feasible, which is the theater of everyday politics theorized as "the art of the possible" cannot address the challenges confronting humanity or fragments of humanity as in circumstances of oppression, occupation, and servitude. From this perspective, a dedication to what seems impossible from a realistic perspective, is in truth the only realism with emancipatory potential. It provides the only alternative to the sullen acceptance of the intolerable. In a global historical sense, this insight is most vividly appreciated by the inability of the powers that be to solve the challenges of nuclear weaponry and climate change that imperil the future of human civilization and even species survival, illustrating the impotence of reason in the face of such challenges.

In this regard, Žižek controversially examines prominent past failures, despite their hideous character, as what he calls wrong steps in the right direction, including Stalinism, Maoism, even revolutionary terror. He quotes approvingly the provocation of Samuel Beckett: "Ever tried. Ever failed. Try again. Fail again. Fail Better,"[6] which for Žižek contrasts with the prevailing posture of "indifference" toward the human condition that "drowns us deeper in the morass of imbecilic Being."[7] The courage to embark on a utopian project of the sort associated with revolutionary movements even with its experience of disillusionment and failure contains what Žižek calls "a redemptive moment" because it displays the willingness to struggle and even die on behalf of a better human future, and without such a willingness, we humans now seem doomed to become an extinct species in the not too distant future.

To summarize up to this point. The embrace of lost causes is not what it seems to be so long as we reject the cynical realism or skeptical wisdom of my French diplomat. In effect, since we never know what the future holds, and much that once seemed impossible has happened, no worthy cause is definitively lost. Related to this affirmation is the idea that dedication to a noble cause, whether viewed as lost or not, is itself individually and collectively redemptive. Further, is the realization that the history of struggle for true freedom and justice despite being obstructed by the brutal forces of reaction, needs to continue. Without such aspirations and struggle the world and we in the world are lost. Goethe expressed this thought in the patriarchal language of his day: "Him who strives he we may save." It is also the destiny of Sisyphus consigned to push a heavy boulder forever up the side of a mountain, knowing that near the top it will fall back again to the bottom and the process must be repeated over and over. When Albert Camus informs us that we can imagine Sisyphus "happy" with this destiny, it is also conveying a pessimistic version of this insight—that the best we can hope for in life is to strive and struggle for what is better even if while doing so we have the awareness that failure is inevitable and hope irrelevant, that Sisyphus is living out a life sentence in pursuit of a truly lost cause.

When Said turns in the middle of his Tanner Lecture from literature to his own existential connection with the theme of lost causes, his comments are worth reflecting upon. He asks two preliminary questions:

> What if we try to grapple with lost causes in the public political world where efforts on behalf of causes actually take place? Is there the same ironized inevitability there, or do subjective hope and renewed effort make a lost cause something to be refused as defeatism?[8]

Said here poses in the abstract the crucial issue as to whether what is noble in literature becomes ethically unacceptable in the life-world of political struggle. He personalizes this issue, saying: "Here I can do no better than to offer my personal experience as a politically active Palestinian as evidence, particularly as these have crystallized since the watershed Oslo agreement of September 1993."[9]

It is worth pausing to note that 1993 was what I would call the second awakening of Edward Said in relation to the Palestinian national movement.

The first is well known, the impact of the 1967 War, shifting Said's primary identity from immersion in his professional role as prominent literary critic to an embrace of an activist role as the world's leading public intellectual espousing the Palestinian cause. In other words, it was at the moment of what appeared to be the most humiliating political and military Palestinian defeat that Said decides to devote mind and heart to the Palestinian struggle, thereby refusing the practical wisdom of the French diplomat earlier mentioned. Less well known is his 1993 turning point, when Said's mounting skepticism about the directions of PLO leadership reached a negative climax in reaction to the Oslo events that most non-Palestinians at the time hailed as a breakthrough for peace. In my view, it was his judgment that Arafat and the PLO leadership by agreeing to a diplomatic framework at Oslo that was slanted heavily toward Israel had effectively surrendered and accepted an arrangement that amounted to a defeatist admission that the Palestinian struggle had indeed become "a lost cause" in the falsely definitive sense. Said resigned from the Palestinian National Council (PNC), and pointedly refused to walk down this path of defeatism. More than 20 years later, the principled wisdom of his position, is finally being widely acknowledged. I interpret the vote in the British House of Commons in favor of recognizing Palestinian statehood as a belated and still somewhat ambiguous recognition of the futility of relying on the Oslo approach. Oslo insisted that only through negotiations could Palestinians hope to move toward becoming a state, and by symbolically circumventing such a framework, the British Parliament was conveying the idea that it was unreasonable to deny Palestinian statehood any longer. As Omar Barghouti and others have pointed out, although the gesture was welcome, it means nothing if not reinforced by the recognition and realization of Palestinian rights as self-determined.

Said to explain his different phases of engagement with the Palestinian cause contrasts the resurgent nationalism that occurred after the 1967 experience with the defeatist diplomacy pursued leading up to and following from 1993. Indicting the PLO defeatism, Said observes that: "it seemed neither appropriate nor really possible to see ourselves in terms of other dispossessed and forgotten peoples like the Armenians, American Indians, Tasmanians, gypsies, and Australian aborigines."[10] Putting aside his controversial, and I believe mistaken presumption that these defeated peoples are also "forgotten," his Archimedian point of contrast is illuminating: "On the contrary, we modeled ourselves on the Vietnamese people, whose resistance to U.S. intervention seemed exactly what we should undertake,"[11] and was coupled with the acknowledged inspiration he received from the writing of Frantz Fanon and the exploits of General Võ Nguyên Giáp. It is crucial to understand that the "we" in Said's phrasing was a reference to the Palestinian people of his persuasion and not to the leaders who represent Palestine on the global diplomatic stage.

From the perspective of "lost causes," Said's choice of Fanon and Vietnam is illuminating. As already mentioned, the Vietnamese were somehow able to turn their totally lost cause on the battlefield, being completely dominated by American military superiority, into a miracle of political victory. This capacity of resilience and perseverance, what Palestinians call *sumud*, on the part of the peoples of the South during their struggle against Western colonial rule is a reality that the United States and Israel have yet to appreciate as borne out by their sequence of failed interventions in the period since the 9/11 attacks in the Arab world and Afghanistan, and now ISIS. For Said, this commitment to the Palestinian lost cause was globalized: "We saw ourselves as a Third World people, subjected to colonialism and oppression, now undertaking our own self-liberation from domination as well as the liberation of our territory."[12] In a later passage, he faults the Palestinians for falling into the tactical and propaganda trap set by their adversaries of being perceived as "terrorists," which he contends never was the true ethos of the movement. He insists that the Palestinian movement was and should remain secular and democratic in its essential ambition, and thus profoundly different from the politics elsewhere in the region, which he considers post-nationalist and oriented around some form of Islam. He believed that the Palestinian outlook was "a distinct advance over those of the Arab states, with their oligarchies, military dicta-torships, brutal police regimes."[13] So the question he confronted was whether as a Palestinian he should adopt a hopeful or defeatist view of what presented itself as a lost cause, and in opting for a hope against hope, he was challenging "the lostness" of the Palestinian lost cause while the PLO in opting for Oslo was agreeing to swallow the bitter pill of defeat and its resulting humiliation of permanent subjugation in their own homeland.

Said addresses this challenge of apparent defeat and the accompanying feelings of hopelessness both in literature and in relation to the Palestinian situation, and gives a very different answer than my French ambassador. In effect, he turns away from this prevalent kind of worldly realism as irrelevant, and affirms that the only true choice is between surrender and resistance. He chooses resistance, or put differently, declares a refusal to accept the unacceptable however unfavorable "the facts on the ground" had become. In so doing, Said inverts this sinister formula Israel frequently invokes. It is used to obtain a grudging acceptance by Washington of these de facto realities that are the result of trampling upon Palestinian rights under international law.

So as to appreciate Said's rejection of Oslo as a framework for peace, it is necessary to consider what was wrong about it from a Palestinian viewpoint. I would point to five features:

1. the fragmentation of the West Bank into Areas A, B, and C making untenable territorial coherence during the period of occupation;
2. the idea that Palestinian goals could only be achieved on the basis of Israeli consent, despite the UN Security Council having already in 1967 unanimously mandated a withdrawal from the territory occupied during the 1967 War;
3. the designation of the United States as the permanent intermediary for these negotiations despite its partisan alignment with Israel, which already was in the driver's seat from a diplomatic perspective;
4. and maybe most important of all, the exclusion of international law and the authority of the UN from the negotiating process, which was the Palestinian trump in their political deck of cards. International law was clearly on the side of the Palestinians in relation to their main claims and grievances. These included border, refugees, settlements, Jerusalem, and water, as well as the day-to-day practices associated with the occupation. Without the inclusion of Palestinian rights under international law, diplomacy degenerates into a bargaining process, which ensures that power disparities will be embodied in any negotiated solution and a heavily slanted

one-sided outcome in Israel's favor would be falsely proclaimed as "peace."

Even Palestinian objections to continuing Israeli settlement expansion as "unlawful" were rebuffed by Washington as unhelpful obstructions to the supposed peace process; the Palestinian humiliation was most vividly expressed by their acceptance of the 1993 Declaration of Principles that did not even refer to Palestine's inalienable right of self-determination;

5. the perverse deepening of such an exclusion by acquiescing in Israel's unlawful activities as was validated outside the negotiating framework by George W. Bush's letter to Ariel Sharon in April 2004 to the effect that the US Government agrees that any end to the conflict must include the incorporation of the settlement blocs into Israeli territory; Hillary Clinton, while Obama's Secretary of State, added to this hegemonic sanitation of illegality calling the settlement phenomenon "subsequent developments" that must be acknowledged by the Palestinians if they sought peace.

The unreasonableness of the deconstructed Oslo approach as a means to achieve a just peace is accentuated in my view by the prior unheralded forthcomingness of the PLO in its endorsement of the 1988 PNC decision to recognize Israel within 1967 borders. Such a bold unilateral initiative, supported by Said when announced, renounced the PLO's earlier refusal to accept the existence of Israel in any form, and exhibited a willingness to swallow a territorial arrangement that accorded the Palestinians only 22 percent of historic Palestine. As is well known, this was less than half of what the UN in its partition plan of 1947 had offered, which at the time seemed grossly unfair given the relative size of the Jewish and Palestinian populations. The fact that such a unilateral diplomatic initiative by the Palestinians failed to yield any acknowledgement at all from Israel, much less some sort of reciprocal gesture raises doubts as to whether even the then far more moderate leadership in Tel Aviv was ever really interested in achieving a two-state solution. This was it seems despite giving verbal assurances to the contrary over the years while at the same time taking a variety of steps that made the possibility less and less attractive to the Palestinians.

These elements of the overall situation are descriptive of the defeatist period of the Palestinian inter-governmental posture that seemed ready to settle for arrangements that disregarded Palestinian rights under international law. There was considerable anxiety among Palestinian intellectuals surrounding the Clinton initiative in 2000 that Arafat might make a deal that accepted the settlements and relinquished the rights of several million Palestinian refugees. In fact, the Second Intifada was interpreted as a warning to the PLO as well as a rebuff of Israel. There were further disquieting developments in this Oslo period: massive settlement expansion; a refusal by Israel to respect the 2004 International Court of Justice findings calling for the dismantling of the Separation Wall; an apartheid structure of occupation in the West Bank; a process of incremental ethnic cleansing in East Jerusalem; and a harsh regime of collective punishment imposed on Gaza that featured three Israeli campaigns of state terror against a caged population in the course of the last six years. These attacks on Gaza of warlike ferocity that were unprecedented in locking the civilian population into the combat zone, disallowing even women and children to claim refugee status by crossing the border or seeking secure sanctuary within Gaza. Yet these dispiriting realities are far from the whole story of Palestinian resistance and struggle. The formal leadership of Palestine may have taken the defeatist route, but Palestinians as a people kept their faith, by and large, in the necessity of resistance and of not giving up their long quest for a sustainable and just peace.

We need to remember that Said rejected the defeatist interpretation of the Palestinian lost cause, and in the process transferred his energies from the bankruptcy of top-down diplomacy to the empowering potential of bottom-up people oriented civil society militancy. This shift can be situated most dramatically in 1987, the time of the First Intifada, a mobilization of Palestinian resistance that was nonviolent, yet withheld all forms of cooperation from the occupier. It was reinforced by the Second Intifada in 2000 that was again in part a populist reaction to Israeli policies, but lacked the nonviolent discipline of the earlier uprising. In 2005, a joint appeal from 170 Palestinian civil societies to launch a global Boycott, Divestment, and Sanctions Campaign with its own defined political goals was a step toward resituating the national Palestinian movement. It represented a further shift in the direction of civil society leadership and toward a movement of global solidarity that has been gaining momentum in the last couple of years. This momentum was further accelerated by the moral outrage generated by the Israeli 50-day attack on Gaza that commenced in July 2014, which seemed especially strong in Western Europe.

What seemed a defining moment in 1993 has now been superseded by a recent cluster of events to creating a new defining moment in 2014, which involves a reformulation of perceptions in relation to the Palestinian struggle. In some ways the situation from the Palestinian perspective has never seemed darker, undoubtedly making the cynical realist write off of the conflict more prevalent:

- the direct talks between Israel and the Palestinian Authority exhibited a total lack of commitment by the Netanyahu government to any solution that ended the occupation of the West Bank and East Jerusalem; the collapse of these talks confirms the futility of the Oslo approach. This posture is reinforced by the latest readings of Israeli public opinion. The respected Jerusalem Center for Public Affairs released a poll in October 2014[14] showing that over 75 percent of Israel's citizens oppose the creation of a Palestinian state on the 1967 borders (even with settlement blocs incorporated), they oppose the withdrawal from the Jordan Valley in a peace agreement even if international peacekeeping forces replace the IDF now deployed there, and they oppose the division of Jerusalem; this suggests that even if Israel's government truly sought a peace agreement that accords with the two-state mantra, the Israeli public would repudiate it;

- in July 2014, the Israeli Knesset elected Reuven Rivlin as the tenth President of Israel, an outspoken advocate of incorporating the whole of the West Bank into Israel, along with Jerusalem, and implementing an Israeli one-state solution that fulfills the maximalist version of the Zionist Project; Rivlin, unlike Netanyahu, believes that oppression of the Palestinians should be eased provided that they agree to live in law-abiding peace within a Jewish state that would once and for all extinguish Palestinian political dreams;

- distressingly, the Arab countries were passive accomplices in support of Israel's attack on Gaza in July 2014, in pursuit of their own agendas that called for the destruction of any grass-roots Islamically oriented political actor in the region—an approach that followed from their ardent support for General Sisi's coup in Egypt against the democratically elected Muslim Brotherhood leadership;

- Israeli public opinion was, according to the Israeli peace activist and political figure, Uri Avnery, 99 percent behind the fury of the 2014 attacks; others noted high-level and populist incitements to genocide during Protective Edge, with numerous unrepudiated statements calling for the destruction and elimination of civilian society as a whole in Gaza; the vivid testimony given in September 2014 at the Russell Tribunal by the Israeli journalist, David Sheen,[15] provides persuasive documentation of the incitement charges;
- once more Gaza was devastated by attacks that killed more than 2,100 Palestinians, injured another 11,000, and traumatized the entire population, which was locked in the combat zone with no means to cross a border to become a refugee or to seek safety internally;
- and the US Congress remains as unconditionally committed to Israel as ever, despite some signs of discomfort at the White House, which seems to want to sustain the credibility of the Oslo approach against all the evidence that Israel uses periodic negotiations for delay and propaganda, and that Palestine loses time and territory.

This pattern of developments reveals an Israel facing little diplomatic pressure to resolve the conflict by negotiations, and no incentive of its own to do so. For Palestine, there exists only a fragile unity between the PLO and Hamas, and a debilitating dependence on Israel and the United States for the funds needed to maintain order in territories under their administrative control. Yet in the face of this, in one of the most brilliant Palestinian analysts of the conflict, Ali Abunimah writes these startling sentences at the very beginning his fine book, *The Battle for Justice in Palestine*: "The Palestinians are winning. This might seem like hubris or even insensitivity. After all, in so many ways things have never looked worse."[16] We must ask what does Abunimah mean by winning, and what basis can he have for being hopeful while being keenly aware of the dire situation facing the Palestinians.

Abunimah is, in effect, telling my French diplomat to look deeper at the overall picture if he wants to understand the reality of the situation.

"It is not a matter of how long you look that matters, but what you see." What should we see?

There are a few factors to consider: the discrediting of Oslo; the growth of the global solidarity movement; the moves toward Palestinian political unity; the recognition of Israeli criminality and American complicity as increasing pressure on the Palestinian Authority to take their complaint to the International Criminal Court; growing evidence that Israel is more worried about what it calls "the delegitimation project" than about the threats posed by Palestinian armed resistance; and finally, the upsurge of regional extremism in the Middle East that could at some point undermine Israel's security.

What Abunimah sees that the realist's blinkered vision misses are the legitimacy and psycho-political dimensions of conflict in our post-colonial world. These dimensions center on the powerful mobilizing impact on a population of a denial of its inalienable right to self-determination and other elemental rights. This is particularly so, as in the Palestinian case, if the denial rests on colonialist patterns of occupation that are partially sustained by links to geopolitical actors, in this instance, the United States. Such a denial of rights creates a deep awareness of "illegitimacy" that is further heightened by Israel's defiance of international law, UN authority, and universal standards of morality. It strengthens the political will of Palestinians to engage in resistance, and creates a climate that encourages more militant forms of global solidarity. This interplay of national resistance and a supportive global public opinion, manifested by various kinds of activism, is what turned the tide against European colonialism throughout the world. So far the Zionist Movement, aided by a unique set of historical circumstances, has succeeded in swimming against this nationalist tide in the global South. It should be observed that this historical trend should not be confused with the struggles of national self-determination against native autocracies. Chechnya, Tibet, and the regimes that have emerged in the Middle East after the Arab Spring do not support the rose-tinted view that democracy, human rights, and economic well-being are part of the anti-colonial narrative as to the flow of history. Furthermore, these victories over European colonialism neither produced benign national governments from the perspective of human rights, democracy, and social justice nor did these nationalist victories neutralize the economic, diplomatic, and cultural roles of global hegemonic forces led by the United States in many national contexts.

Let me end with two clusters of conclusions:

- The Palestinian struggle remains a lost cause in the French sense so long as the Oslo approach of reducing Palestinian representation to "moderate" forces, excluding Hamas, and endowing the United States with the role of impartial mediator constitutes the peace process. As welcome as were the Swedish and House of Commons initiatives on Palestinian statehood, they were ambiguous to the extent that they justified their initiatives as support for "moderate" Palestinians who could revive direct negotiations leading to a two-state solution. In effect, the message being sent is "Oslo is dead, long live Oslo." These so-called moderates in Ramallah have proved themselves incapable of producing a sustainable and just peace, and if this is to happen, it must reflect the will of the Palestinian people not their unrepresentative leaders, and it must not remain locked with a two-state mantra that has been made irrelevant by the passage of time.

- The Palestinian struggle is more than ever a lost cause in the uplifting Edward Said sense of being centered on a commitment to Palestinian self-determination achieved by Palestinian resistance reinforced by a global solidarity movement. This Palestinian resistance in its latest phase has gained momentum by relying primarily on nonviolent tactics of increasing militancy, and by rejecting the defeatist notion that the moderate voice of the Palestinian Authority speaks for the Palestinian people as a whole. This Palestinian public consensus also, by and large, rejects the view that Hamas speaks for the Palestinian people, despite Hamas's recent popularity even in secular circles due to their resilience and resistance in the face of Israel's recent campaign of state terrorism. This second commitment to the Palestinian lost cause is politically premised on the realization that people throughout the world have demonstrated historical agency in relation to the right of self-determination and especially in relation to European colonialism. Such a resolve also includes accepting what Said so often insisted upon—that achieving Palestinian rights should never be realized through a second dispossession, this time dispossessing the Jewish presence in historic Palestine. In effect, this presupposes a Palestinian acceptance of the core Zionist idea of "a Jewish homeland" while rejecting both the notion of "a Jewish state" and the maximalist Zionist view currently being implemented that such a state should include the whole of historic Palestine, including the West Bank and Jerusalem. It is a hopeful sign that the Palestinian civil society consensus is also explicit in accepting a permanent Jewish presence in historic Palestine under these terms.

Let me end, then, with a reaffirmation of the complex relationship between our limited knowledge, especially of the future, and our political and moral will, that has the irreducible freedom to create its own horizons. It is for this reason alone that it seems empowering to join with Edward Said and Žižek in declaring our defense of lost causes, in this instance that of the Palestinian people who have endured an unspeakable ordeal of victimization for so long. As in South Africa where in the end the racist white elites were able to remain after the collapse of the apartheid regime, it will take a comparable political miracle to reach a just and sustainable peace in Palestine that upholds the equal dignity of both peoples. In this spirit, I end with the enigmatic plea of the poet, W.H. Auden: "We who are about to die demand a miracle."

Notes

2. Oslo Diplomacy: A Legal Historical Perspective

1. See Caroline Frank, "Rabin's Assassination: The Story that Changed the Nation," *Jerusalem Post Magazine*, November 4, 2014; "Rabin's Death was Netanyahu's Victory: An Explosive New Film Argues that Bibi is Morally Culpable for the 1995 Assassination," *Salon*, June 30, 2016.

2. Ehud Olmert of the Kadima Party became prime minister in 2006; he continued the Sharon approach, and then lost the leadership role when the Likud Party was victorious in 2009, and Netanyahu was chosen to again lead the Israeli government.

3. See Edward W. Said, *The End of the Peace Process: Oslo and After* (New York: Pantheon, 2000); for more recent advocacy of one-state solutions, see Ali Abunimah, *One Country: A Bold Proposal to End the Israeli–Palestinian Conflict* (New York: Metropolitan Books, 2006); and Saree Makdisi, *Palestine Inside Out: An Everyday Occupation* (New York: W.W. Norton, 2008).

4. It had long been believed that Israel launched a pre-emptive war in 1967 because of its reasonable apprehension of an attack by its Arab neighbors, which understandingly led to widespread support for the Israeli victory. For a very convincing refutation of this bit of conventional wisdom on the 1967 War, see the well-sourced study by John Quigley, *The Six-Day War and Israeli Self-Defense: Questioning the Legal Basis for Preventive War* (Cambridge: Cambridge University Press, 2013).

5. I tried to argue along these lines in Richard Falk, "International Law and the Peace Process," *Hastings International and Comparative Law Review* (2005), 28(3): 421–447.

6. See International Court of Justice, "Legal Consequences of the Construction of a Wall in the Occupied Palestinian Territory: Advisory Opinion," July 9, 2004, www.icj-cij.org/docket/files/131/1671.pdf.

7. See Clayton E. Swisher (ed.), *The Palestine Papers: The End of the Road* (Chatham: Hesperus Press, 2011).

8. John Quigley, *The Statehood of Palestine: International Law in the Middle East Conflict* (Cambridge: Cambridge University Press, 2011).

9. Said, *The End of the Peace Process*, Note 2, at xii.

3. Rethinking the Palestinian Future

1. A very revised version of presentation at the National Second Annual Conference of Research Centers in the Arab World, Doha, Qatar, December 7–9, 2013, "The Palestinian Cause and the Future of the Palestinian Movement."

2. See Rashid Khalidi, *Brokers of Deceit: How the US has Undermined Peace in the Middle East* (Boston, MA: Beacon Press, 2013).

3. Jeremy R. Hammond, *Obstacle to Peace: The US Role in the Israeli–Palestinian Conflict* (Cross Village, MI: Worldview Publications, 2015).

4. See The White House, Press Office, "Remarks of President Barack Obama to the People of Israel," March 21, 2013, www.whitehouse.gov/the-press-office/2013/03/21/remarks-president-obama-people-Israel.

5. Ibid.

6. Ibid.

7. For more details on the American Israel Public Affairs Committee (AIPAC)—America's Pro-Israel Lobby, see www.aipac.org/about/mission.

8. See Amira Hass, "The Inner Syntax of Palestinian Stone-Throwing," *Haaretz*, April 3, 2013, and Amira Hass, "Broken Bones and Broken Hopes," *Haaretz*, November 4, 2005; and see also Gideon Levy, "The Inner Syntax of the Storm," *Haaretz*, April 7, 2013, www.haaretz.com/opinion/the-inner-syntax-of-the-storm.premium-1.513860.

9. Edward W. Said, *The Question of Palestine* (New York: Times Books, 1979), 235.

10. Jabotinsky's main argument was based on his belief that only by force could the Zionist goals be achieved, a strategy summarized by the metaphor "iron wall," which has inspired Israeli hardliners, giving rise to the Likud Party that has governed Israel in most recent years. For elaboration, see Avi Shlaim, *The Iron Wall: Israel and the Arab World* (New York: W.W. Norton, 2001).

11. As quoted by Goldmann in Nahum Goldmann, *The Jewish Paradox* (New York: Grosset & Dunlap, 1978), 99.

4. The Emergent Palestinian Imaginary

1. Henry Siegman was the Executive Director of the American Jewish Congress (1978–1994) and has been one of the most prominent and influential critics of Israel's recent policy toward the Palestinians and of its move toward ethnocracy. For a comprehensive discussion

of ethnocracy in the Israel–Palestine context, see Oren Yiftachel, "'Ethnocracy': the Politics of Judaising Israel/Palestine," *Constellations: International Journal of Critical and Democratic Theory* (1998) 6(3), 364–390.

5. Violence and Nonviolence in the Palestinian Human Rights Struggle

1. In his 2009 "Cairo Speech," Obama stated that:

   Palestinians must abandon violence. Resistance through violence and killing is wrong and it does not succeed. For centuries, black people in America suffered the lash of the whip as slaves and the humiliation of segregation. But it was not violence that won full and equal rights. It was a peaceful and determined insistence upon the ideals at the center of America's founding. This same story can be told by people from South Africa to South Asia; from Eastern Europe to Indonesia.

   Barack Obama, "Remarks by the President on a New Beginning," Cairo University, Egypt, June 4, 2009.

2. Mazin Qumsiyeh, *Popular Resistance in Palestine: A History of Hope and Empowerment* (London: Pluto, 2011), 229; Wendy Pearlman, *Violence, Nonviolence and the Palestinian National Movement* (Cambridge: Cambridge University Press, 2011).

3. Ronit Avni, "From Budrus to Bilin: Arresting Heroes," *Huffington Post*, October 15, 2010, www.huffingtonpost.com/ronit-avni/from-budrus-to-bilin-arre_b_763613.html.

4. Gene Sharp, *The Role of Power in Nonviolent Struggle* (Boston, MA: Albert Einstein Institute, 1990); Gene Sharp, *The Politics of Nonviolent Action* (Boston, MA: Porter Sargent, 1973); Johan Galtung, *Nonviolence and Israel/Palestine* (Honolulu, HI: University of Hawaii Institute for Peace, 1989).

5. Cited in Stephen Moss, "Arundhati Roy: 'They are Trying to Keep Me Destabilized: Anybody Who Says Anything is in Danger'," *Guardian*, June 5, 2010.

6. Erica Chenoweth and Maria Stephan, *Why Civil Resistance Works: The Strategic Logic of Nonviolent Conflict* (New York: Columbia University Press, 2011).

7. Ibid.

8. Maria Stephan and Erica Chenoweth, "Why Civil Resistance Works: The Strategic Logic of Nonviolent Conflict," *International Security* (2008), 33(1), 8.

9. Chenoweth and Stephan, *Why Civil Resistance Works*, 16–17.

10. Stephan and Chenoweth, "Why Civil Resistance Works," 9–10; Gene Sharp, *Waging Nonviolent Struggle: 20th Century Practice and 21st Century Potential* (Boston, MA: Porter Sargent, 2005).

11. Stephan and Chenoweth, "Why Civil Resistance Works," 10; Sharp, *Waging Nonviolent Struggle*.

12. Chenoweth and Stephan, *Why Civil Resistance Works*; Sharon Erickson Nepstad and Lester Kurtz, "Introduction," in Sharon Erickson Nepstad and Lester Kurtz (eds), *Nonviolent Conflict and Civil Resistance* (Bingley: Emerald, 2012).

13. Chenoweth and Stephan, *Why Civil Resistance Works*; Erickson Nepstad and Kurtz, "Introduction."

14. Sharp, *The Politics of Nonviolent Action*, 64.

15. Stephan and Chenoweth, "Why Civil Resistance Works," 9–10.

16. See, for example, Matthew Eddy, "When your Gandhi is Not My Gandhi: Memory Templates and Limited Violence in the Palestinian Human Rights Movement," in Sharon Erickson Nepstad and Lester Kurtz (eds), *Nonviolent Conflict and Civil Resistance* (Bingley: Emerald, 2012), 185–211.

17. Pearlman, *Violence, Nonviolence*, 3–4.

18. Chenoweth and Stephan, *Why Civil Resistance Works*, 12–13.

19. Ibid., 12.

20. Sharp, *The Role of Power*, 15.

21. Qumsiyeh, *Popular Resistance in Palestine*, 241; Oliver Ramsbotham, Tom Woodhouse, and Hugh Miall, *Contemporary Conflict Resolution* (London: Polity, 2011).

22. Ilan Pappe, *A History of Modern Palestine* (Edinburgh: Edinburgh University Press, 2003), 1–136.

23. Edward Kaufman and Ibrahim Bisharat, "Introducing Human Rights into Conflict Resolution: The Relevance for the Israeli–Palestinian Peace Process," *Journal of Human Rights* (2002), 1(1), 88; Jacob Shamir and Khalil Shikaki, *Palestinian and Israeli Public Opinion: The Public Imperative in the Second Intifada* (Bloomington, IN: Indiana University Press, 2010).

24. Galtung, *Nonviolence and Israel–Palestine*; Sharp, *The Politics of Nonviolent Action*.

25. Ibid.

26. Chenoweth and Stephan, *Why Civil Resistance Works*, 30–61.

27. Ibid.

28. Maxine Kaufman-Lacusta, *Refusing to be Enemies: Palestinian and Israeli Nonviolent Resistance to the Israeli Occupation* (Reading: Ithaca, 2011).

29. Galtung, *Nonviolence and Israel–Palestine*; Sharp, *The Politics of Nonviolent Action*.

30. Chenoweth and Stephan, *Why Civil Resistance Works*, 50–61.

31. Ibid.

32. Ibid.; Andrew Rigby, *Palestinian Resistance: Nonviolence* (Jerusalem: PASSIA: Palestine Academy for Study of International Affairs, 2010), 68–69.

33. Erickson Nepstad and Kurtz, "Introduction," xvi–xvii.

34. International Court of Justice (ICJ), "Legal Consequences of the Construction of a Wall in the Occupied Palestinian Territory: Advisory Opinion," July 9, 2004, www.icj-cij.org/docket/files/131/1671.pdf; Richard Falk, "International Law and Palestinian Resistance," in Joel Beinin and Rebecca L. Stein (eds), *The Struggle of Sovereignty: Palestine and Israel, 1993–2005* (Stanford, CA: Stanford University Press, 2006), 315–23.

35. ICJ, "Legal Consequences of the Construction of a Wall."

36. Falk, "International Law," 315–23; UN Human Rights Council, "Human Rights in Palestine and Other Occupied Arab Territories," September 25, 2009, http://www2.ohchr.org/english/bodies/hrcouncil/docs/12session/A-HRC-12-48.pdf; Amnesty International, "Israel/Gaza: Operation 'Cast Lead': 22 Days of Death and Destruction," July 2, 2009, www.amnesty.org/en/documents/MDE15/015/2009/en/; Human Rights Watch, "Rain of Fire: Israel's Unlawful Use of White Phosphorus in Gaza," March 25, 2009, www.hrw.org/report/2009/03/25/rain-fire/israels-unlawful-use-white-phosphorus-gaza.

37. Ibrahim Shikaki, "What is the 'Right' Type of Resistance?" *Al Jazeera*, June 6, 2011.

38. Lizzy Dearden, "Ban Ki-moon says Wave of Violence in Israel and the West Bank 'Bred from Decades of Israeli Occupation,'" *The Independent*, December 20, 2015, www.independent.co.uk/news/world/middle-east/ban-ki-moon-says-wave-of-violence-in-israel-and-the-west-bank-bred-from-decades-of-israeli-a6779811.html.

39. See, for example, Pearlman, *Nonviolence, Violence*; Lori Allen, Salim Tamar and Issam Nassar, "Palestinians Debate 'Polite' Resistance to Occupation," in Joel Beinin and Rebecca L. Stein (eds), *The Struggle of Sovereignty: Palestine and Israel, 1993–2005* (Stanford, CA: Stanford University Press, 2006), 288–302.

40. Pearlman, *Violence, Nonviolence*; Yezid Sayigh, *Armed Struggle and the Search for State: The Palestinian National Movement, 1949–1993* (Oxford: Oxford University Press, 1999).

41. Within Palestinian society the term *shahid* has historically referred to anyone killed by the enemy. In the West, however, the term has become synonymous with what Palestinians instead call *istishhadi*, people who undertake "martyrdom" operations such as suicide bombings against the enemy. Nasser Abufarhar, *The Making of a Human Bomb: An Ethnography of Palestinian Resistance* (Durham, NC: Duke University Press, 2009).

42. Robert Pape, *Dying to Win: The Strategic Logic of Suicide Terrorism* (New York: Random House, 2005); Shaul Mishal and Avraham Sela, *The Palestinian Hamas: Vision, Violence, and Coexistence* (New York: Columbia University Press, 2000).

43. Abufarhar, *Making of a Human Bomb*. Likewise, there have been examples where Israelis have rejoiced at the suffering of Palestinians, such as when groups of Israelis gathered on hilltops near the Gaza border to celebrate the bombing of Gaza in July 2014. Harriet Sherwood, "Israelis Gather on Hillsides to Watch and Cheer as Military Drops Bombs on Gaza," *Guardian*, July 20, 2014.

44. Qumsiyeh, *Popular Resistance in Palestine*, 233–234.

45. Arieh O'Sullivan, "The Slow Turn Towards Palestinian Non-Violence," *The American Taskforce on Palestine*, February 14, 2012.

46. Ibid.

47. Ibid. Also see Shikaki, "What is the 'Right' Type of Resistance?"

48. Michael Broning, *The Politics of Change in Palestine: State-Building and Non-Violent Resistance* (London: Pluto Press, 2011), 134.

49. Hanan Ashrawi, "Palestine and the Arab Spring," *Carnegie Endowment for Peace*, May 27, 2011.

50. Pearlman, *Violence, Nonviolence*, 1; Mary Elizabeth King, *A Quiet Revolution: The First Palestinian Intifada and Nonviolent Resistance* (New York: Nation Books, 2007), 50–52 and 92; Rigby, *Palestinian Resistance*, 7–30.

51. Qumsiyeh, *Popular Resistance in Palestine*, 229. Also see Broning, *The Politics of Change in Palestine*, 134–135; Pearlman, *Violence, Nonviolence*, 27–61.

52. Until recently, the standard narrative surrounding the events of 1948 was that the dispossession of Palestinians was the result of Palestinian leaders ordering their people to flee the situation, and the "collateral damage" that came with the wider conflict. However, as uncovered by the so-called Israeli "Revisionist Historians," a considerable amount of the refugee flow resulted from offensive tactics by Zionists to gain as much land as possible for the fledgling Jewish state, including through a deliberate policy of "transfer" of Palestinians. See Ilan

Pappe, *The Ethnic Cleansing of Palestine* (Oxford: One World, 2006), 40; Avi Shlaim, *The Iron Wall: Israel and the Arab World* (New York: W.W. Norton, 2001), 28–53; Benny Morris, *The Birth of the Palestinian Refugee Problem* (Cambridge: Cambridge University Press, 1988).

53. Rigby, *Palestinian Resistance*, 41–42.

54. Susan Akram "Myths and Realities of the Palestinian Refugee Problem: Reframing the Right of Return," in Susan Akram, Michael Dumper, Michael Lynk, and Iain Scobbie (eds), *International Law and the Israeli–Palestinian Conflict* (London: Routledge, 2011), 1 and 28–29.

55. Rigby, *Palestinian Resistance*, 43–45.

56. Sara Roy, *Failing Peace: Gaza and the Palestinian–Israeli Conflict* (London: Pluto Press, 2007); Souad Dajani, *Eyes Without Country: Searching for a Palestinian Strategy of Liberation* (Philadelphia, PA: Temple University Press, 1994), 13–26; Cheryl A. Rubenberg, "Twenty Years of Israeli Economic Policies in the West Bank and Gaza: Prologue to the Intifada," *Journal of Arab Affairs* (1989) 8(1), 28–73; Pappe, *A History of Modern Palestine*, 202–203; Rigby, *Palestinian Resistance*, 46–50.

57. Pearlman, *Violence, Nonviolence*, 95–101; Rigby, *Palestinian Resistance*, 46–50.

58. Rigby, *Palestinian Resistance*, 46–50.

59. Pearlman, *Violence, Nonviolence*, 95–101; Broning, *Politics of Change*; Dajani, *Eyes Without Country*; Pappe, *A History of Modern Palestine*, 183–228.

60. Sayigh, *Armed Struggle*, 309; John Cooley, *Green March, Black September: The Story of the Palestinian Arabs* (London: Frank Cass, 1973), 125–130.

61. Khalidi, *Brokers of Deceit*, 10–11; Edward Said, "The Essential Terrorist," *The Nation*, August 14, 2006; Tomis Kapitan, "The Terrorism of 'Terrorism,'" in James Sterba (ed.), *Terrorism and International Justice* (Oxford: Oxford University Press, 2003), 57–59.

62. Qumsiyeh, *Popular Resistance in Palestine*, 228; Said, "The Essential Terrorist"; Ilan Pappe, "The Inevitable War on Terror: De-Terrorising the Palestinians," in Alex Houen (ed.), *States of War Since 9/11: Terrorism, Sovereignty and the War on Terror* (Abingdon: Routledge, 2014), 84–102.

63. Zachary Lockman and Joel Beinin (eds), *Intifada: The Palestinian Uprising Against Israeli Occupation* (London: I.B. Tauris, 1990); Don Peretz, *Intifada: The Palestinian Uprising* (Boulder, CO: Westview Press, 1990); Rigby, *Palestinian Resistance*, 51–55.

64. King, *A Quiet Revolution*, 1 and 109–126; Joost Hilterman, *Behind the Intifada: Labor and Women's Movements in the Occupied Territories*, (Princeton, NJ: Princeton University Press, 1991), 215; Chenoweth and Stephan, *Why Civil Resistance Works*, 119.

65. Graham Usher, "Children of Palestine," *Race & Class* (April/June 1990) 32(4).

66. Edward Kaufman, "The Intifada's Limited Violence," *Journal of Arab Affairs* (1990) 9(2).

67. Ibid.

68. Shikaki, "What is the 'Right' Type of Resistance?" See also Amira Hass, "The Inner Syntax of Palestinian Stone-Throwing," *Haaretz*, April 3, 2013; Maia Carter Hallward, *Transnational Activism and the Israeli–Palestinian Conflict* (New York: Palgrave Macmillan, 2013), 50.

69. Lockman and Beinin, *Intifada*; Peretz, *Intifada*.

70. Shlaim, *The Iron Wall*, 453–454.

71. Amira Hass, "Broken Bones and Broken Hopes," *Haaretz*, November 4, 2005; Wendy Pearlman, *Violence, Nonviolence*, 114; Chenoweth and Stephan, *Why Civil Resistance Works*, 129; Shlaim, *The Iron Wall*, 453; Lockman and Beinin, *Intifada*.

72. Broning, *The Politics of Change in Palestine*, 136–137; Lockman and Beinin, *Intifada*.

73. Shlaim, *The Iron Wall*, 598–599.

74. Ibid.

75. Kauffman, "The Intifada's Limited Violence"; Shlaim, *The Iron Wall*, 453.

76. Rigby, *Palestinian Resistance*, 52–53.

77. Ibid.; Peretz, *Intifada*, 163–193.

78. Chenoweth and Stephan, *Why Civil Resistance Works*, 129.

79. Ibid., 130.

80. Ibid.

81. Stephen Zunes, "Unarmed Resistance in the Middle East and North Africa," in Stephen Zunes, Lester R. Kurtz, and Sarah Beth Asher, (eds), *Nonviolent Social Movements: A Geographical Perspective* (Malden, MA: Blackwell, 1999), 48.

82. Jeroen Gunning, *Hamas in Politics: Democracy, Religion, Violence* (New York: Columbia University Press, 2009), 203–207; Kaufman and Bisharat, "Introducing Human Rights"; Rigby, *Palestinian Resistance*, 59.

83. Gunning *Hamas in Politics*; Pearlman, *Violence, Nonviolence*, 136–149; Ehud Sprinzak, *Brother Against Brother: Violence and Extremism in*

Israeli Politics from Altalena to the Rabin Assassination (New York: Free Press, 1999), 217–286.

84. Ilan Pappe, "Clusters of History: US Involvement in the Palestine Question," *Race & Class* (2007) 48(3), 21; Rigby, *Palestinian Resistance*, 59–62.

85. Khalidi, *Brokers of Deceit*. For example, as Amnesty International note, the provisions of Oslo for access to water supplies has resulted in a situation whereby:

> access to water resources by Palestinians in the OPT is controlled by Israel and the amount of water available ... is restricted to a level which does not meet their needs and does not constitute a fair and equitable share of the shared water resources.

Amnesty International, *Troubled Waters: Palestinians Denied Fair Access to Water* (London: Amnesty International Publications, 2009).

86. Miloon Kothari, "Economic, Social and Cultural Rights: Report of the Special Rapporteur," Commission on Human Rights, E/CN4/2003/5/Add.1, June 12, 2002, 5.

87. As Jeroen Gunning explains, between 1994 and 2000, an average of three suicide bombings a year was carried out by Hamas and Islamic Jihad, see Gunning, *Hamas in Politics*, 208.

88. Pearlman, *Violence, Nonviolence*, 127–149; Rigby, *Palestinian Resistance*, 63; Chenoweth and Stephan, *Why Civil Resistance Works*, 137.

89. Maia Carter Hallward and Julie M. Norman (eds), *Nonviolent Resistance in the Second Intifada: Activism and Advocacy* (New York: Palgrave Macmillan, 2011).

90. Broning, *The Politics of Change in Palestine*, 137; Daniel Byman, *A High Price: The Triumphs and Failures of Israeli Counterterrorism* (Oxford: Oxford University Press, 2011), 124; Reuven Pedatzur, "More than a Million Bullets," *Haaretz*, June 29, 2004.

91. See, for example, Pearlman, *Violence, Nonviolence*, 150–186; Rigby, *Palestinian Resistance*, 63–65; for a timeline of the events, see Ramzy Baroud, *The Second Palestinian Intifada: A Chronicle of a People's Struggle* (London: Pluto Press, 2006), 168–195.

92. Martin Asser, "Lynch Mob's Brutal Attack," *BBC Online*, October 13, 2000.

93. "Intifada Toll 2000–2005," *BBC News*, February 8, 2005.

94. O'Sullivan, "The Slow Turn."

95. Hallward and Norman, *Nonviolent Resistance*, 6–8; Rigby, *Palestinian Resistance*, 66–67; Allen, Tamari, and Nasser "Palestinians Debate 'Polite' Resistance," 292–293; Pearlman, *Violence, Nonviolence*, 163.

96. Seth Ackerman, "Al-Aqsa Intifada and the U.S. Media," *Journal of Palestine Studies* (2001) 30(2), 61–74; Edward Said, "Palestinians Under Siege," in Roane Carey (ed.), *The New Intifada: Resisting Israel's Apartheid* (London: Verso, 2001), 31.

97. Conal Urquhart, "Hamas in Call to End Suicide Bombings," *Guardian*, April 9, 2006.

98. See contributions to Hani Faris (ed.), *The Failure of the Two State Solution: The Prospects of One State in the Israel–Palestine Conflict* (London: I.B. Tauris, 2013).

99. UN Office for the Coordination of Humanitarian Affairs Occupied Palestinian Territory (UNOCHA), *Fragmented Lives: Humanitarian Overview* (East Jerusalem: May 2012), www.ochaopt.org/documents/ocha_opt_fragmented_lives_annual_report_2012_05_29_english.pdf.

100. ICJ, "Legal Consequences."

101. Ibid.; UNOCHA, *Fragmented Lives*.

102. Avni, "From Budrus to Bilin."

103. Ibid.

104. Saed Bannoura, "Army Attacks Weekly Protests Against the Wall, Injuries Reported," *International Middle East Media Centre*, November 5, 2011.

105. Avni, "From Budrus to Bilin."

106. Broning, *The Politics of Change in Palestine*, 141.

107. B'Tselem, *Human Rights in the Occupied Territories: Annual Report 2007* (Jerusalem, January 2008).

108. Jonathan Kuttab cited in Kauffman, "The Intifada's Limited Violence"; Shikaki, "What is the 'Right' Type of Resistance?"

109. Kate Shuttleworth, "Palestinian Stone Throwers Could Face 20 Years in Jail," *Guardian*, November 4, 2014.

110. Dalia Hatuqa, "Israel Jails Palestinian Girl, 14, for Throwing Stone," *Al Jazeera*, January 26, 2015; Patrick Strickland, "Israeli Courts Convict Hundreds of Palestinian Children," *Al Jazeera*, April 10, 2015.

111. Roni Schocken, "Chilling Effect of the Nakba Law on Israel's Human Rights," *Haaretz*, May 17, 2012.

112. B'Tselem, *Human Rights in the Occupied Territories*.

113. Ibid.

114. Ibid.

115. For a more detailed assessment of Palestinian hunger strikes in 2011–2012, see Richard Falk, *Palestine: The Legitimacy of Hope* (Washington, DC: Just World Books, 2014), 79–114.

116. Al Jazeera, "Israel Authorizes Force-Feeding of Prisoners," July 30, 2015, www.aljazeera.com/news/2015/07/israel-authorises-force-feeding-prisoners-150730064042746.html.

117. O'Sullivan, "The Slow Turn."

118. Ashrawi, "Palestine and the Arab Spring," 20.

119. Carlo Strenger, "Israel's Extreme Right isn't Jewish, it's Totalitarian," *Haaretz*, December 20, 2015, www.haaretz.com/opinion/.premium-1.692846; Zeev Sternhell, "The Obligation of a True Patriot," *Haaretz*, February 19, 2010; Brent Sasley, "Israel's Right-Turn: Behind Bibi's Victory," *Foreign Affairs*, March 24, 2015; Noam Sheizaf, "The Triumph of the Far Right in Israel," *The Nation*, January 28, 2013; Stephen Lendman, "Israel on a Fast Track to Depotism," *Baltimore Chronicle*, October 12, 2012; Carlo Strenger, "Loyalty Oath is not about Arabs, It's about Hatred of Liberal Values," *Haaretz*, October 11, 2010; Gideon Levy, "The Jewish Republic of Israel," *Haaretz*, October 10, 2010.

120. Barak Ravid, "Netanyahu: If I'm Elected, There will be no Palestinian State," *Haaretz*, March 16, 2015; *Haaretz*, "Lieberman: Disloyal Israeli Arabs Should be Beheaded," March 9, 2015; Jill Reilly, "Israeli Official Calls for Concentration Camps in Gaza and 'the Conquest of the Entire Gaza Strip, and Annihilation of all Fighting Forces and their Supporters,'" *Daily Mail*, August 4, 2014; Mira Bar Hillel, "Why I'm on the Brink of Burning my Israeli Passport," *Independent*, July 11, 2014.

121. Neve Gordon, "From Colonization to Separation: Exploring the Structure of Israel's Occupation," *Third World Quarterly* (2008) 29(1), 26; Gideon Levy, "Meet the Israelis," *Haaretz*, October 25, 2012; Oren Yiftachel, "From Fragile 'Peace' to Creeping Apartheid: Notes on the Recent Politics of Israel/Palestine," *Arena Journal, New Series* (2001) 16(1), 22; Karl Vick, "Why Israel Doesn't Care About Peace," *Time*, September 2, 2010.

122. Ibid.

123. Barak Ravid and Jack Khoury, "EU, U.S. State Department Condemn 'Vicious' West Bank Arson Attack," *Haaretz*, July 31, 2015.

124. See, for example, the Israeli journalist Avi Issacharoff's account of a similar attack he witnessed in 2008: "The Killing of Ali Saad Dawabsha will not be the Last," *The Times of Israel*, July 31, 2015, www.timesofisrael.com/the-killing-of-ali-saad-dawabsha-will-not-be-the-last/.

125. Al Jazeera, "Israelis Protest Hate Crimes in Wake of Baby's Death," August 2, 2015.

126. Kate Shuttleworth, "Family Members of Toddler in Critical Condition after West Bank Arson Attack," *Guardian*, August 2, 2015.

127. Ilan Ben Zion and Judah Ari Gross, "Israel Arrests Jewish Terror Suspects in Deadly Firebombing," *Haaretz*, December 3, 2015; "At Least Four Detained Jewish Terror Suspects Have Dual Citizenship," *Haaretz*, December 18, 2015, www.haaretz.com/israel-news/1.692599 ?v=6997819AF3554A0F0848AAF639E8596C.

128. Dearden, "Ban Ki-moon says Wave of Violence"; James North and Philip Weiss, "In 'NYT' Coverage of Violence, Only Jewish Victims Count," *Mondoweiss,* October 4, 2015 (updated), http://mondoweiss. net/2015/10/coverage-violence-victims.

129. Amnesty International (AI), *Israel and the Occupied Palestinian Territories: 2014/15 Annual Report*; Human Rights Watch (HRW) *Israel Palestine: World Report 2014*; B'Tselem, *Human Rights in the Occupied Palestinian Territories: 2014 Annual Report*; B'Tselem, *Settler Violence: The Nature of the Violence*, undated; Breaking the Silence, *This is How we Fought in Gaza: Soldier's Testimonies and Photographs from Operation "Protective Edge" 2014*, Tel Aviv, 2015.

130. "Sessions," Russell Tribunal on Palestine, www.russelltribunalon palestine.com/en/sessions.

131. Barbara Harlow, "Apartheid or not Apartheid? The Russell Tribunal on Palestine, South Africa Session, November 2011," *Law, Culture & the Humanities* (October 2013) 9(3), 412–420.

132. Rigby, *Palestinian Resistance*, 66–67.

133. "About ISM," International Solidarity Movement website, http:// palsolidarity.org/about/.

134. "Gaza: The Killing Zone," Dispatches, Channel 4 (UK), May 22, 2003; Matthew Kalman, "Israeli Inquiry into Rachel Corrie Death Insufficient, US Ambassador Tells Family," *Guardian*, August 25, 2012; Sean O'Hagan, "A Remarkable Man's Photographs of the Middle East," *Guardian*, March 1, 2012.

135. Freedom Flotilla Coalition, https://freedomflotilla.org/about. For an in-depth discussion of the blockade, see UNOCHA, "The Gaza Strip: The Humanitarian Impact of the Blockade," July 2015, www.ochaopt. org/documents/ocha_opt_gaza_blockade_factsheet_july_2015_ english.pdf.

136. See "Report of the Secretary-General's Panel of Inquiry on the 31 May 2010 Flotilla Incident," September 2011, www.un.org/News/ dh/infocus/middle_east/Gaza_Flotilla_Panel_Report.pdf (more colloquially known as the "Palmer Report"); "Israeli Action Against Gaza Flotilla 'Unlawful'—UN Human Rights Council Panel," UN

News Centre, September 23, 2010, www.un.org/apps/news/story.
asp?NewsID=36086#.VZiJr_knKTo.

137. See, for example, Rachel Giora, "Supporting the Palestinian BDS
Movement from Within," *Boycott Israel*, January 18, 2010, http://
boycottisrael.info/content/milestones-history-israeli-bds-movement-
brief-chronology; "Gaza Aid Flotilla: Henning Mankell Calls for
Sanctions on Israel," *Telegraph*, June 2, 2010; Neve Gordon, "Boycott
Israel: An Israeli comes to the Painful Conclusion that it's the Only
Way to Save his Country," *Los Angeles Times*, August 20, 2009;
"Letter: Over 100 Artists Announce a Cultural Boycott of Israel,"
Guardian, February 14, 2015; Harriet Sherwood and Matthew Kalman,
"Stephen Hawking Joins Academic Boycott of Israel," *Guardian*, May
8, 2013; Alison Flood, "Alice Walker Declines Request to Publish
Israeli Edition of The Color Purple," *Guardian*, June 20, 2012; Vikram
Dodd and Rory McCarthy, "Elvis Costello Cancels Concerts in Israel
in Protest at Treatment of Palestinians," *Guardian*, May 19, 2010.

138. Desmond Tutu, "My Plea to the People of Israel: Liberate Yourselves
by Liberating Palestine," *Haaretz*, August 14, 2014.

139. "Introducing the BDS Movement," BDS website, www.bdsmovement.
net/bdsintro; Omar Barghouti, *Boycott, Divestment, Sanctions: The
Global Struggle for Palestinian Rights* (Chicago, IL: Haymarket Books,
2011); Audrea Lim (ed.) *The Case for Sanctions Against Israel* (London:
Verso, 2012); Ilan Pappe, *Out of the Frame: The Struggle for Academic
Freedom in Israel* (London: Pluto Press, 2010), 194–197.

140. See, for example, Peter Beaumont, "Israel Brands Palestinian-Led
Boycott Movement A 'Strategic Threat,'" *Guardian*, June 3, 2015,
www.theguardian.com/world/2015/jun/03/israel-brands-palestin-
ian-boycott-strategic-threat-netanyahu; Judy Maltz, "Alan Dershowitz:
BDS a Strategic Threat to Israel in the Long Term," *Haaretz*, June 10,
2014; Neve Gordon, *Israel's Occupation* (Berkeley, CA: University of
California Press, 2008), 189–191.

141. Judith Butler, *Precarious Life: The Powers of Mourning and Violence*
(London: Verso, 2004), 101–127; Beaumont, "'Strategic Threat'";
Pappe, *Out of the Frame*; Alan Brownfeld, "Boycotting Israel is not
anti-Semitism," *Washington Post*, June 13, 2015; Richard Falk, "Two
Types of Anti-Semitism," *Global Justice in the 21st Century* blog,
September 1, 2014, https://richardfalk.wordpress.com/2014/09/01/
two-types-of-anti-semitism/.

142. Ibid.

143. "Introducing," BDS website; Barghouti, *Boycott, Divestment, Sanctions*;
Lim (ed.) *The Case for Sanctions*.

144. Hanan Ashrawi, "Is a Boycott of Israel Just?" *New York Times*, February 18, 2014.

145. Jack Moore, "Bill Gates Criticized for Investment in G4S' Israel Torture Prisons," *International Business Times*, April 17, 2014; Gill Plimmer, "UK Watchdog to Probe G4S Israeli Contract," *Financial Times*, June 2, 2014; Laurie Goodstein, "Presbyterians Vote to Divest Holdings to Pressure Israel," *New York Times*, June 20, 2014; Barak Ravid, "Kerry: Israel Risks Turning into an 'Apartheid State,'" *Haaretz*, April 28, 2014.

146. Guardian, "Over 100 Artists"; Sherwood and Kalman, "Stephen Hawking"; Amanda Holpuch, "US Churches Vote on Joining BDS Movement Against Israel," *Guardian*, July 1, 2015; Chris McGreal, "Sheldon Adelson looks to Stamp Out Growing US Movement to Boycott Israel," *Guardian*, June 6, 2015.

147. Rory McCarthy, "Suspend Military Aid to Israel, Amnesty Urges Obama after Detailing US Weapons used in Gaza," *Guardian*, February 23, 2009.

148. "Here Comes Your Non-Violent Resistance," *The Economist*, May 17, 2011.

6. International Law, Apartheid, and Israeli Responses to BDS

1. International Convention on the Suppression and Punishment of the Crime of Apartheid, was adopted by the General Assembly of the United Nations on November 30, 1973, https://treaties.un.org/doc/Publication/UNTS/Volume%201015/volume-1015-I-14861-English.pdf.

2. The Rome Statute of the International Criminal Court is the treaty that established the International Criminal Court (ICC); it entered into force on July 1, 2002.

3. For elaboration, my report to the UN General Assembly, "Report of the Special Rapporteur on the situation of human rights in the Palestinian Territories occupied since 1967," August 30, 2010, see especially paragraph 5 on apartheid features of the occupation.

4. See International Court of Justice, "Legal Consequences of the Construction of a Wall in the Occupied Palestinian Territory, Advisory Opinion," July 9, 2004, www.icj-cij.org/docket/files/131/1671.pdf.

5. "The Balfour Declaration," November 2, 1917.

6. The Reut Institute, "The BDS Movement Promotes the Delegitimation of the State of Israel," June 10, 2010.

7. The Reut Institute, "The Delegitimization Challenge: Creating a Political Firewall," February 14, 2010.

8. Ibid.

9. From private conversation with the author.

10. Reut Institute, "The Delegitimation Challenge."

11. It is correct that the Palestinians attempted in the 1980s a form of hard power globalization of their struggle via a variety of violent tactics including the hijacking of planes and ships, shootings in public places, and seizing hostages at Olympic Games.

    Such tactics did expand the battlefield, but alienated world public opinion and involved relying on unlawful attacks on civilians, and were abandoned.

12. The Goldstone Report, the United Nations Fact Finding Mission on the Gaza Conflict, was a fact-finding team established by the UN Human Rights Commission after the Gaza attack ended in January 2009. For the text of report and commentary, see Adam Horowitz, Lizzy Ratner, and Philip Weiss (eds), *The Goldstone Report: The Legacy of the Landmark Investigation of the Gaza Conflict* (New York: Nation Books, 2011).

13. Reut Institute, "The BDS Movement."

14. For effective responses to these lines of criticism of BDS, see Omar Barghouti, *Boycott, Divestment, Sanctions: The Global Struggle for Palestinian Rights* (Chicago, IL: Haymarket Books, 2011), 143–150.

15. See the helpful exposition of law by Joel Greenberg, "Israeli Anti-Boycott Law Stirs Debate on Settlement Products," *Washington Post*, July 22, 2011. For commentary, see Lahav Harkov, "Anti-Boycott Bill Becomes Law after Passing Knesset," *Jerusalem Post*, November 7, 2011.

16. Ibid.; also statement of Human Rights Watch, "Israel: Anti-Boycott Bill Stifles Expression," July 13, 2011, www.hrw.org/en/news/2011/07/13/Israel-anti-boycott-bill-stifles-expression?print.

17. In May and June Palestinian activists, joined by some international supporters, sought to reclaim their right of return on the anniversaries of the *Nabka* (1948) and *Naksa* (1967), and were met by Israeli lethal violence resulting in more than 40 deaths and hundreds of injuries. Israel's excessive use of force was condemned by the Special Envoy of the UN Secretary General to the Middle East. For a helpful account, see Khalid Amayreh, "The Second Intifada—An Israeli Strategy," *Al Jazeera* English, August 12, 2009.

7. Palestinian Law and the Search for a Just Peace

1. See the Report of "International Fact-Finding Mission on Israeli Settlements in the Occupied Palestinian Territory," UN Human Rights

Council, January 31, 2013; for a helpful interpretation, see Harriet Sherwood, "Israel Must Withdraw all Settlers or Face ICC," *Guardian*, January 31, 2013.

8. Palestine Becomes a State

1. "Abbas' Speech to the UN General Assembly, November 2012," *Council on Foreign Relations*, November 29, 2012, www.cfr.org/palestine/abbas-speech-un-general-assembly-november-2012/p29579.
2. See "UN General Assembly Resolution A/67/L.28, Palestine," *Council on Foreign Relations*, November 29, 2012, www.cfr.org/palestine/un-general-assembly-resolution-67l28-palestine/p29574.
3. For text of Susan Rice's statement at the UN, see "Susan Rice's Statement on Palestine's UN Status, November 29, 2012," *Council on Foreign Relations*, November 29, 2012, www.cfr.org/palestine/susan-rices-statement-palestines-un-status-november-2012/p29575.
4. See the Report of "International Fact-Finding Mission on Israeli Settlements in the Occupied Palestinian Territory," UN Human Rights Council, January 31, 2013.

9. Seeking Vindication at the International Criminal Court

1. Ali Weinberg, "Why Palestinians Joining International Court Could Scuttle Peace Talks," *ABC News*, April 2, 2014, http://abcnews.go.com/blogs/politics/2014/04/palestinians-could-take-more-unilateral-actions-ambassador-to-un-says/.

10. Zionism and the United Nations

1. Speeches by Ambassadors Herzog and Moynihan to the UN General Assembly, November 10, 1975, which were outraged responses to the passage of UN General Assembly Resolution 3379 on the same day that condemned Zionism as a form of racism.
2. For a fuller exposition, see Glenn Greenwald's interview, "Interview with BDS Co-Founder Omar Barghouti: Banned by Israel from Traveling, Threatened with Worse," *The Intercept*, May 13, 2016.

11. The US State Department, the Definition of Anti-Semitism, and Edward Said's Humanism

1. For elaboration, see Noam Chomsky, "The Responsibility of Intellectuals," in *American Power and the New Mandarins* (New York:

Random House, 1967), 323–359; Edward W. Said, *Representations of the Intellectual* (New York: Random House, 1996).

2. Timothy Snyder, *Black Earth: The Holocaust as History and Warning* (New York: Tim Duggan Books, 2015).

3. *Contemporary Anti-Semitism: A Report Provided to the U.S. Congress*, U.S. Department of State, n.d.; See also fact sheet of U.S. Department of State, June 8, 2010, on defining anti-Semitism.

4. Michael Oren, *Ally: My Journey Across the American–Israeli Divide* (New York: Random House, 2015).

5. Akeel Bilgrami, *Secularism, Identity, and Enchantment* (Cambridge, MA: Harvard University Press, 2014).

6. Edward W. Said, *The Question of Palestine* (New York: Vintage Edition, 1992 [1979]).

7. Edward W. Said, *Orientalism* (New York: Pantheon, 1978), xxvii.

8. Edward W. Said, *Power, Politics, and Culture* (New York: Pantheon, 2001), 446.

9. Said, *Orientalism*, xxviii.

10. Ibid., 27.

11. Both quotes from Said, *The Question of Palestine*, 59.

12. Said, *Orientalism*, xxii.

13. Edward W. Said, *Representations of the Intellectual* (New York: Pantheon, 1994), xvi.

12. The Failed Peace Process: A Prophetic Indictment

1. See Elias Khoury in Müge Gürsoy Sökmen and Başak Ertür (eds), *Waiting for the Barbarians: A Tribute to Edward Said* (London: Verso, 2008).

2. Edward W. Said, *The Question of Palestine* (New York: Vintage (1992 [1979]), vii.

3. For Henry Siegman's views, see "Israel's Lies," *London Review of Books*, January 29, 2009.

4. Ibid.

5. For example, see Ilan Pappe, *The Ethnic Cleansing of Palestine* (Oxford: One World, 2006).

6. Gauri Viswanathan (ed. and intro), *Power, Politics, and Culture: Interviews with Edward W. Said* (New York: Vintage, 2002), 446; note that Ari Shavit seems to move in this direction in his *My Promised Land: The Triumph and Tradgey of Israel* (New York: Spiegel & Grau, 2015).

7. Viswanathan, *Power, Politics, and Culture*, 435.

8. Ibid., 456.

13. Palestine as a "Lost Cause"

1. All references in chapter are to the essay titled "On Lost Causes," published in Edward W. Said, *Reflections on Exile and Other Essays* (Cambridge, MA: Harvard University Press, 2000), 527–553.
2. Said, "On Lost Causes," 533.
3. Ibid., 527–528.
4. Slavoj Žižek, *In Defense of Lost Causes* (London: Verso, 2008), 2.
5. Ibid., 2.
6. Samuel Beckett, "Worstward Ho," novella, 1983.
7. Žižek, *In Defense of Lost Causes*, 7.
8. Said, "On Lost Causes," 542.
9. Ibid.
10. Ibid., 543.
11. Ibid.
12. Ibid., 546.
13. Ibid., 547.
14. Jerusalem Center for Public Affairs, "New Poll: 75% of Israeli Jews Oppose a Palestinian State on the 1967 Lines, Israeli Withdrawal from the Jordan Valley, and the Division of Jerusalem," October 19, 2014, http://jcpa.org/poll-israeli-jews-oppose-palestinian-state/.
15. See "The Gaza War (2014) under International Law: An Inquiry into Israel's Crimes, Responsibility, and the Response of the International Community," Russell Tribunal on Palestine, Brussels, September 25, 2014, www.russelltribunalonpalestine.com/en/wp-content/uploads/2014/09/Summary-of-findings-1.pdf.
16. Ali Abunimah, *The Battle for Justice in Palestine* (Chicago, IL: Haymarket Books, 2014).

References

Abufarhar, Nasser (2009) *The Making of a Human Bomb: An Ethnography of Palestinian Resistance*. Durham, NC: Duke University Press.

Abunimah, Ali (2006) *One Country: A Bold Proposal to End the Israeli–Palestinian Conflict*. New York: Metropolitan Books.

Abunimah, Ali (2014) *The Battle for Justice in Palestine*. Chicago, IL: Haymarket Books.

Ackerman, Seth (2001) "Al-Aqsa Intifada and the U.S. Media," *Journal of Palestine Studies* 30(2), 61–74.

Akram, Susan (2011) "Myths and Realities of the Palestinian Refugee Problem: Reframing the Right of Return," in Susan Akram, Michael Dumper, Michael Lynk, and Iain Scobbie (eds), *International Law and the Israeli–Palestinian Conflict*. London: Routledge.

Al Jazeera (2015) "Israel Authorizes Force-Feeding of Prisoners," July 30.

Al Jazeera (2015) "Israelis Protest Hate Crimes in Wake of Baby's Death," August 2.

Allen, Lori, Tamar, Salim, and Nassar, Issam (2006) "Palestinians Debate 'Polite' Resistance to Occupation," in Joel Beinin and Rebecca L. Stein (eds), *The Struggle of Sovereignty: Palestine and Israel, 1993–2005*. Stanford, CA: Stanford University Press, 288–302.

Amayreh, Khalid (2009) "The Second Intifada—An Israeli Strategy," *Al Jazeera English*, August 12.

Amnesty International (2009) "Israel/Gaza: Operation 'Cast Lead': 22 Days of Death and Destruction," July 2, www.amnesty.org/en/documents/MDE15/015/2009/en/.

Amnesty International (2009) *Troubled Waters: Palestinians Denied Fair Access to Water*. London: Amnesty International Publications.

Amnesty International (2014) *Israel and the Occupied Palestinian Territories: 2014/15 Annual Report*.

Ashrawi, Hanan (2011) "Palestine and the Arab Spring," *Carnegie Endowment for Peace*, May 27.

Ashrawi, Hanan (2014) "Is a Boycott of Israel Just?" *New York Times*, February 18.

Asser, Martin (2000) "Lynch Mob's Brutal Attack," *BBC Online*, October 13.

Avni, Ronit (2010) "From Budrus to Bilin: Arresting Heroes," *Huffington Post*, October 15, www.huffingtonpost.com/ronit-avni/from-budrus-to-bilin-arre_b_763613.html.

Bannoura, Saed (2011) "Army Attacks Weekly Protests Against the Wall, Injuries Reported," *International Middle East Media Centre*, November 5.

Barghouti, Omar (2011) *Boycott, Divestment, Sanctions: The Global Struggle for Palestinian Rights*. Chicago, IL: Haymarket Books.

Bar Hillel, Mira (2014) "Why I'm on the Brink of Burning my Israeli Passport," *Independent*, July 11.

Baroud, Ramzy (2006) *The Second Palestinian Intifada: A Chronicle of a People's Struggle*. London: Pluto Press.

Beaumont, Peter (2015) "Israel Brands Palestinian-Led Boycott Movement A 'Strategic Threat,'" *Guardian*, June 3.

Ben Zion, Ilan and Ari Gross, Judah (2015) "Israel Arrests Jewish Terror Suspects in Deadly Firebombing," *Haaretz*, December 3.

Bilgrami, Akeel (2014) *Secularism, Identity, and Enchantment*. Cambridge, MA: Harvard University Press.

Broning, Michael (2011) *The Politics of Change in Palestine: State-Building and Non-Violent Resistance*. London: Pluto Press.

Brownfeld, Alan (2015) "Boycotting Israel is not anti-Semitism," *Washington Post*, June 13.

B'Tselem (2008) *Human Rights in the Occupied Territories: Annual Report 2007*. Jerusalem, January.

B'Tselem (2014) *Human Rights in the Occupied Palestinian Territories: 2014 Annual Report*.

B'Tselem (2015) *Settler Violence: The Nature of the Violence*, undated; Breaking the Silence, *This is How we Fought in Gaza: Soldier's Testimonies and Photographs from Operation "Protective Edge" 2014*, Tel Aviv.

Butler, Judith (2004) *Precarious Life: The Powers of Mourning and Violence*. London: Verso.

Byman, Daniel (2011) *A High Price: The Triumphs and Failures of Israeli Counterterrorism*. Oxford: Oxford University Press.

Chenoweth, Erica and Stephan, Maria (2011) *Why Civil Resistance Works: The Strategic Logic of Nonviolent Conflict*. New York: Columbia University Press.

Chomsky, Noam (1967) "The Responsibility of Intellectuals," in *American Power and the New Mandarins*. New York: Random House.

Cooley, John (1973) *Green March, Black September: The Story of the Palestinian Arabs*. London: Frank Cass.

Dearden, Lizzy (2015) "Ban Ki-moon says Wave of Violence in Israel and the West Bank 'Bred from Decades of Israeli Occupation,'" *The Independent*,

December 20, www.independent.co.uk/news/world/middle-east/ban-ki-moon-says-wave-of-violence-in-israel-and-the-west-bank-bred-from-decades-of-israeli-a6779811.html.

Dodd, Vikram and McCarthy, Rory (2010) "Elvis Costello Cancels Concerts in Israel in Protest at Treatment of Palestinians," *Guardian*, May 19.

Economist (2011) "Here Comes Your Non-Violent Resistance," *Economist*, May 17.

Eddy, Matthew (2012) "When your Gandhi is Not My Gandhi: Memory Templates and Limited Violence in the Palestinian Human Rights Movement," in Sharon Erickson Nepstad and Lester Kurtz (eds), *Nonviolent Conflict and Civil Resistance*. Bingley: Emerald, 185–211.

Erickson Nepstad, Sharon and Kurtz, Lester (eds) (2012) *Nonviolent Conflict and Civil Resistance*. Bingley: Emerald.

Falk, Richard (2005) "International Law and the Peace Process," *Hastings International and Comparative Law Review* 28(3): 421–447.

Falk, Richard (2006) "International Law and Palestinian Resistance," in Joel Beinin and Rebecca L. Stein (eds), *The Struggle of Sovereignty: Palestine and Israel, 1993–2005*. Stanford, CA: Stanford University Press, 315–323.

Falk, Richard (2014) *Palestine: The Legitimacy of Hope*. Washington, DC: Just World Books.

Falk, Richard (2014) "Two Types of Anti-Semitism," *Global Justice in the 21st Century* blog, September 1, https://richardfalk.wordpress.com/2014/09/01/two-types-of-anti-semitism/.

Faris, Hani (ed.) (2013) *The Failure of the Two State Solution: The Prospects of One State in the Israel–Palestine Conflict*. London: I.B. Tauris.

Flood, Alison (2012) "Alice Walker Declines Request to Publish Israeli Edition of The Color Purple," *Guardian*, June 20.

Frank, Caroline (2014) "Rabin's Assassination: The Story that Changed the Nation," *Jerusalem Post Magazine*, November 4.

Galtung, Johan (1989) *Nonviolence and Israel/Palestine*. Honolulu, HI: University of Hawaii Institute for Peace.

Giora, Rachel (2010) "Supporting the Palestinian BDS Movement from Within," *Boycott Israel*, January 18, http://boycottisrael.info/content/milestones-history-israeli-bds-movement-brief-chronology.

Goldmann, Nahum (1978) *The Jewish Paradox*. New York: Grosset & Dunlap.

Goodstein, Laurie (2014) "Presbyterians Vote to Divest Holdings to Pressure Israel," *New York Times*, June 20.

Gordon, Neve (2008) "From Colonization to Separation: Exploring the Structure of Israel's Occupation," *Third World Quarterly* 29(1), 25–44.

Gordon, Neve (2008) *Israel's Occupation*. Berkeley, CA: University of California Press.

Gordon, Neve (2009) "Boycott Israel: An Israeli comes to the Painful Conclusion that it's the Only Way to Save his Country," *Los Angeles Times*, August 20.

Greenberg, Joel (2011) "Israeli Anti-Boycott Law Stirs Debate on Settlement Products," *Washington Post*, July 22.

Greenwald, Glenn (2016) "Interview with BDS Co-Founder Omar Barghouti: Banned by Israel from Traveling, Threatened with Worse," *The Intercept*, May 13.

Guardian (2015) "Letter: Over 100 Artists Announce a Cultural Boycott of Israel," *Guardian*, February 14.

Gunning, Jeroen (2009) *Hamas in Politics: Democracy, Religion, Violence*. New York: Columbia University Press.

Haaretz (2015) "Lieberman: Disloyal Israeli Arabs Should be Beheaded," March 9.

Haaretz (2015) "At Least Four Detained Jewish Terror Suspects Have Dual Citizenship," *Haaretz*, December 18.

Hallward, Maia Carter and Norman, Julie M. (eds) (2011) *Nonviolent Resistance in the Second Intifada: Activism and Advocacy*. New York: Palgrave Macmillan.

Hallward, Maia Carter (2013) *Transnational Activism and the Israeli– Palestinian Conflict*. New York: Palgrave Macmillan.

Hammond, Jeremy R. (2015) *Obstacle to Peace: The US Role in the Israeli– Palestinian Conflict*. Cross Village, MI: Worldview Publications

Harlow, Barbara (2013) "Apartheid or not Apartheid? The Russell Tribunal on Palestine, South Africa Session, November 2011," *Law, Culture & the Humanities* 9(3), 412–420.

Harkov, Lahav (2011) "Anti-Boycott Bill Becomes Law after Passing Knesset," *Jerusalem Post*, November 7.

Hass, Amira (2005) "Broken Bones and Broken Hopes," *Haaretz*, November 4.

Hass, Amira (2013) "The Inner Syntax of Palestinian Stone-Throwing," *Haaretz*, April 3.

Hatuqa, Dalia (2015) "Israel Jails Palestinian Girl, 14, for Throwing Stone," *Al Jazeera*, January 26.

Hilterman, Joost (1991) *Behind the Intifada: Labor and Women's Movements in the Occupied Territories*. Princeton, NJ: Princeton University Press.

Holpuch, Amanda (2015) "US Churches Vote on Joining BDS Movement Against Israel," *Guardian*, July 1.

Horowitz, Adam, Ratner, Lizzy, and Weiss Philip (eds) (2011) *The Goldstone Report: The Legacy of the Landmark Investigation of the Gaza Conflict*. New York: Nation Books.

Human Rights Watch (2009) "Rain of Fire: Israel's Unlawful Use of White Phosphorus in Gaza," March 25, www.hrw.org/report/2009/03/25/rain-fire/israels-unlawful-use-white-phosphorus-gaza.

Human Rights Watch (2011) "Israel: Anti-Boycott Bill Stifles Expression," July 13, www.hrw.org/en/news/2011/07/13/Israel-anti-boycott-bill-stifles-expression?print.

Human Rights Watch (2014) *Israel Palestine: World Report 2014*.

International Court of Justice (ICJ) (2004) "Legal Consequences of the Construction of a Wall in the Occupied Palestinian Territory: Advisory Opinion," July 9, www.icj-cij.org/docket/files/131/1671.pdf.

Issacharoff, Avi (2015) "The Killing of Ali Saad Dawabsha will not be the Last," *The Times of Israel*, July 31, www.timesofisrael.com/the-killing-of-ali-saad-dawabsha-will-not-be-the-last/.

Kalman, Matthew (2012) "Israeli Inquiry into Rachel Corrie Death Insufficient, US Ambassador Tells Family," *Guardian*, August 25.

Kapitan, Tomis (2003) "The Terrorism of 'Terrorism,'" in James Sterba (ed.), *Terrorism and International Justice*. Oxford: Oxford University Press.

Kaufman, Edward (1990) "The Intifada's Limited Violence," *Journal of Arab Affairs* 9(2).

Kaufman, Edward and Bisharat, Ibrahim (2002) "Introducing Human Rights into Conflict Resolution: The Relevance for the Israeli–Palestinian Peace Process," *Journal of Human Rights* 1(1).

Kaufman-Lacusta, Maxine (2011) *Refusing to be Enemies: Palestinian and Israeli Nonviolent Resistance to the Israeli Occupation*. Reading: Ithaca.

Khalidi, Rashid (2013) *Brokers of Deceit: How the US has Undermined Peace in the Middle East*. Boston, MA: Beacon Press.

King, Mary Elizabeth (2007) *A Quiet Revolution: The First Palestinian Intifada and Nonviolent Resistance*. New York: Nation Books.

Kothari, Miloon (2002) "Economic, Social and Cultural Rights: Report of the Special Rapporteur," Commission on Human Rights, E/CN4/2003/5/Add.1, June 12.

Lendman, Stephen (2012) "Israel on a Fast Track to Depotism," *Baltimore Chronicle*, October 12.

Levy, Gideon (2010) "The Jewish Republic of Israel," *Haaretz*, October 10.

Levy, Gideon (2012) "Meet the Israelis," *Haaretz*, October 25.

Levy, Gideon (2013) "The Inner Syntax of the Storm," *Haaretz*, April 7.

Lim, Audrea (ed.) (2012) *The Case for Sanctions Against Israel*. London: Verso.

Lockman, Zachary and Beinin, Joel (eds) (1990) *Intifada: The Palestinian Uprising Against Israeli Occupation*. London: I.B. Tauris.

McCarthy, Rory (2009) "Suspend Military Aid to Israel, Amnesty Urges Obama after Detailing US Weapons used in Gaza," *Guardian*, February 23.

McGreal, Chris (2015) "Sheldon Adelson looks to Stamp Out Growing US Movement to Boycott Israel," *Guardian*, June 6.

Makdisi, Saree (2008) *Palestine Inside Out: An Everyday Occupation*. New York: W.W. Norton.

Maltz, Judy (2014) "Alan Dershowitz: BDS a Strategic Threat to Israel in the Long Term," *Haaretz*, June 10.

Mishal, Shaul and Sela, Avraham (2000) *The Palestinian Hamas: Vision, Violence, and Coexistence*. New York: Columbia University Press.

Moore, Jack (2014) "Bill Gates Criticized for Investment in G4S' Israel Torture Prisons," *International Business Times*, April 17.

Morris, Benny (1988) *The Birth of the Palestinian Refugee Problem*. Cambridge: Cambridge University Press.

Moss, Stephen (2010) "Arundhati Roy: 'They are Trying to Keep Me Destabilized: Anybody Who Says Anything is in Danger'," *Guardian*, June 5.

North, James and Weiss, Philip 2015 (updated) "In 'NYT' Coverage of Violence, Only Jewish Victims Count," *Mondoweiss*, October 4.

Obama, Barack (2009) "Remarks by the President on a New Beginning," Cairo University, Egypt, June 4.

O'Hagan, Sean (2012) "A Remarkable Man's Photographs of the Middle East," *Guardian*, March 1.

Oren, Michael (2015) *Ally: My Journey Across the American–Israeli Divide*. New York: Random House.

O'Sullivan, Arieh (2012) "The Slow Turn Towards Palestinian Non-Violence," *The American Taskforce on Palestine*, February 14.

Pape, Robert (2005) *Dying to Win: The Strategic Logic of Suicide Terrorism*. New York: Random House.

Pappe, Ilan (2003) *A History of Modern Palestine*. Edinburgh: Edinburgh University Press.

Pappe, Ilan (2006) *The Ethnic Cleansing of Palestine*. Oxford: One World.

Pappe, Ilan (2007) "Clusters of History: US Involvement in the Palestine Question," *Race & Class* 48(3).

Pappe, Ilan (2010) *Out of the Frame: The Struggle for Academic Freedom in Israel*. London: Pluto Press.

Pappe, Ilan (2014) "The Inevitable War on Terror: De-Terrorising the Palestinians," in Alex Houen (ed.), *States of War Since 9/11: Terrorism, Sovereignty and the War on Terror*. Abingdon: Routledge, 84–102.

Pearlman, Wendy (2011) *Violence, Nonviolence and the Palestinian National Movement*. Cambridge: Cambridge University Press.

Pedatzur, Reuven (2004) "More than a Million Bullets," *Haaretz*, June 29.

Peretz, Don (1990) *Intifada: The Palestinian Uprising*. Boulder, CO: Westview Press.

Plimmer, Gill (2014) "UK Watchdog to Probe G4S Israeli Contract," *Financial Times*, June 2.

Quigley, John (2011) *The Statehood of Palestine: International Law in the Middle East Conflict*. Cambridge: Cambridge University Press.

Quigley, John (2013) *The Six-Day War and Israeli Self-Defense: Questioning the Legal Basis for Preventive War*. Cambridge: Cambridge University Press.

Qumsiyeh, Mazin (2011) *Popular Resistance in Palestine: A History of Hope and Empowerment*. London: Pluto.

Ramsbotham, Oliver, Woodhouse, Tom, and Miall, Hugh (2011) *Contemporary Conflict Resolution*. London: Polity.

Ravid, Barak (2014) "Kerry: Israel Risks Turning into an 'Apartheid State,'" *Haaretz*, April 28.

Ravid, Barak (2015) "Netanyahu: If I'm Elected, There will be no Palestinian State," *Haaretz*, March 16.

Ravid, Barak and Khoury, Jack (2015) "EU, U.S. State Department Condemn 'Vicious' West Bank Arson Attack," *Haaretz*, July 31.

Reilly, Jill (2014) "Israeli Official Calls for Concentration Camps in Gaza and 'the Conquest of the Entire Gaza Strip, and Annihilation of all Fighting Forces and their Supporters,'" *Daily Mail*, August 4.

Reut Institute (2010) "The Delegitimization Challenge: Creating a Political Firewall," Reut Institute, February 14.

Reut Institute (2010) "The BDS Movement Promotes the Delegitimation of the State of Israel," Reut Institute, June 10.

Rigby, Andrew (2010) *Palestinian Resistance: Nonviolence*. Jerusalem: PASSIA: Palestine Academy for Study of International Affairs.

Said, Edward W. (1978) *Orientalism*. New York: Pantheon.

Said, Edward W. (1992 [1979]) *The Question of Palestine*. New York: Vintage Edition.

Said, Edward W. (1994) *Representations of the Intellectual*. New York: Pantheon.

Said, Edward W. (1996) *Representations of the Intellectual*. New York: Random House.

Said, Edward W. (2000) *The End of the Peace Process: Oslo and After*. New York: Pantheon.

Said, Edward W. (2000) "On Lost Causes," in *Reflections on Exile and Other Essays*. Cambridge, MA: Harvard University Press, 527–553.

Said, Edward (2001) "Palestinians Under Siege," in Roane Carey (ed.), *The New Intifada: Resisting Israel's Apartheid*. London: Verso.

Said, Edward W. (2001) *Power, Politics, and Culture*. New York: Pantheon.

Said, Edward (2006) "The Essential Terrorist," *The Nation*, August 14.

Salon (2016) "Rabin's Death was Netanyahu's Victory: An Explosive New Film Argues that Bibi is Morally Culpable for the 1995 Assassination," *Salon*, June 30.

Sasley, Brent (2015) "Israel's Right-Turn: Behind Bibi's Victory," *Foreign Affairs*, March 24.

Sayigh, Yezid (1999) *Armed Struggle and the Search for State: The Palestinian National Movement, 1949–1993*. Oxford: Oxford University Press.

Schocken, Roni (2012) "Chilling Effect of the Nakba Law on Israel's Human Rights," *Haaretz*, May 17.

Shamir, Jacob and Shikaki, Khalil (2010) *Palestinian and Israeli Public Opinion: The Public Imperative in the Second Intifada*. Bloomington, IN: Indiana University Press.

Sharp, Gene (1973) *The Politics of Nonviolent Action*. Boston, MA: Porter Sargent.

Sharp, Gene (1990) *The Role of Power in Nonviolent Struggle*. Boston, MA: Albert Einstein Institute.

Sharp, Gene (2005) *Waging Nonviolent Struggle: 20th Century Practice and 21st Century Potential*. Boston, MA: Porter Sargent.

Shavit, Ari (2015) *My Promised Land: The Triumph and Tradgey of Israel* (New York: Spiegel & Grau.

Sheizaf, Noam (2013) "The Triumph of the Far Right in Israel," *The Nation*, January 28.

Sherwood, Harriet (2013) "Israel Must Withdraw all Settlers or Face ICC," *Guardian*, January 31.

Sherwood, Harriet (2014) "Israelis Gather on Hillsides to Watch and Cheer as Military Drops Bombs on Gaza," *Guardian*, July 20.

Sherwood, Harriet and Kalman, Matthew (2013) "Stephen Hawking Joins Academic Boycott of Israel," *Guardian*, May 8.

Shikaki, Ibrahim (2011) "What is the 'Right' Type of Resistance?" *Al Jazeera*, June 6.

Shlaim, Avi (2001) *The Iron Wall: Israel and the Arab World*. New York: W.W. Norton.

Shuttleworth, Kate (2014) "Palestinian Stone Throwers Could Face 20 Years in Jail," *Guardian*, November 4.

Shuttleworth, Kate (2015) "Family Members of Toddler in Critical Condition after West Bank Arson Attack," *Guardian*, August 2.

Siegman, Henry (2009) "Israel's Lies," *London Review of Books*, January 29.

Snyder, Timothy (2015) *Black Earth: The Holocaust as History and Warning*. New York: Tim Duggan Books.

Sökmen, Müge Gürsoy and Ertür, Başak (eds) (2008) *Waiting for the Barbarians: A Tribute to Edward Said*. London: Verso, 2008.

Sprinzak, Ehud (1999) *Brother Against Brother: Violence and Extremism in Israeli Politics from Altalena to the Rabin Assassination*. New York: Free Press.

Stephan, Maria and Chenoweth, Erica (2008) "Why Civil Resistance Works: The Strategic Logic of Nonviolent Conflict," *International Security* 33(1), 8.

Sternhell, Zeev (2010) "The Obligation of a True Patriot," *Haaretz*, February 19.

Strenger, Carlo (2010) "Loyalty Oath is not about Arabs, It's about Hatred of Liberal Values," *Haaretz*, October 11.

Strenger, Carlo (2015) "Israel's Extreme Right isn't Jewish, it's Totalitarian," *Haaretz*, December 20.

Strickland, Patrick (2015) "Israeli Courts Convict Hundreds of Palestinian Children," *Al Jazeera*, April 10.

Swisher, Clayton E. (ed.) (2011) *The Palestine Papers: The End of the Road*. Chatham: Hesperus Press.

Telegraph (2010) "Gaza Aid Flotilla: Henning Mankell Calls for Sanctions on Israel," *Telegraph*, June 2.

Tutu, Desmond (2014) "My Plea to the People of Israel: Liberate Yourselves by Liberating Palestine," *Haaretz*, August 14.

UN Human Rights Council (2009) "Human Rights in Palestine and Other Occupied Arab Territories," September 25, http://www2.ohchr.org/english/bodies/hrcouncil/docs/12session/A-HRC-12-48.pdf.

UN News Centre (2010) "Israeli Action Against Gaza Flotilla 'Unlawful' – UN Human Rights Council Panel," UN News Centre, September 23, www.un.org/apps/news/story.asp?NewsID=36086#.VZiJr_knKTo.

UN Office for the Coordination of Humanitarian Affairs Occupied Palestinian Territory (UNOCHA) (2012) *Fragmented Lives: Humanitarian Overview*. East Jerusalem, May, www.ochaopt.org/documents/ocha_opt_fragmented_lives_annual_report_2012_05_29_english.pdf.

UN Office for the Coordination of Humanitarian Affairs Occupied Palestinian Territory (UNOCHA) (2015) "The Gaza Strip: The Humanitarian Impact of the Blockade," July, www.ochaopt.org/documents/ocha_opt_gaza_blockade_factsheet_july_2015_english.pdf.

UN ("Palmer Report") (2011) "Report of the Secretary-General's Panel of Inquiry on the 31 May 2010 Flotilla Incident," September 2011, www.un.org/News/dh/infocus/middle_east/Gaza_Flotilla_Panel_Report.pdf.

Urquhart, Conal (2006) "Hamas in Call to End Suicide Bombings," *Guardian*, April 9.

Usher, Graham (1990) "Children of Palestine," *Race & Class* 32(4).

Vick, Karl (2010) "Why Israel Doesn't Care About Peace," *Time*, September 2.

Viswanathan, Gauri (ed.) (2002) *Power, Politics, and Culture: Interviews with Edward W. Said*. New York: Vintage.

Weinberg, Ali (2014) "Why Palestinians Joining International Court Could Scuttle Peace Talks," *ABC News*, April 2.

White House, Press Office, (2013) "Remarks of President Barack Obama to the People of Israel," March 21, www.whitehouse.gov/the-press-office/2013/03/21/remarks-president-obama-people-Israel.

Yiftachel, Oren (1998) "'Ethnocracy': the Politics of Judaising Israel/Palestine," *Constellations: International Journal of Critical and Democratic Theory* 6(3), 364–390.

Yiftachel, Oren (2001) "From Fragile 'Peace' to Creeping Apartheid: Notes on the Recent Politics of Israel/Palestine," *Arena Journal, New Series* 16(1), 13–25.

Žižek, Slavoj (2008) *In Defense of Lost Causes*. London: Verso.

Zunes, Stephen (1999) "Unarmed Resistance in the Middle East and North Africa," in Stephen Zunes, Lester R. Kurtz, and Sarah Beth Asher, (eds), *Nonviolent Social Movements: A Geographical Perspective*. Malden, MA: Blackwell.

Index